A Keen Wind Blows

The keen wind serves but to brace and harden them; to clear their brains and sweeten their tempers; to purify not only the blood, but surely to help, in so far as we can be helped by such agencies, to purify also their hearts.

Clem Cotterill, Fettes' first Second Master, 1886.

A KEEN WIND BLOWS

The Story of Fettes College

Robert Philp

James X James

First published in 1998
© Fettes College 1998
ISBN 0 907383 85 8

Designed by Susannah May
Printed and bound by Butler & Tanner Limited, Frome, Somerset

Published by
James & James (Publishers) Ltd
Gordon House Business Centre
6 Lissenden Gardens
London NW5 1LX

Picture Acknowledgements

Aberdeen University Library 23; Squadron Leader Bruce Blanche of the Royal Auxiliary Air Force 63 (bottom); *The Cliff Dwellers* 55 (bottom), 56 (top) and 84 (top); *Conference and Common Room* 121; *Illustrated London News* 6; *The Lighter Side of School Life*, Ian Hay, T. N. Foulis 47; *The Scotsman* 76 (top), 83, 89; *You Only Live Twice*, Ian Fleming, Hodder 78. General photographs of the School by Ralph Hughes, Andrew Murray and Emma Riley.

Half-title page: *Old Fettesian 2nd XI v. School 2nd XI, 1888.*

Frontispiece: *Fettes in the 1870s from Queensferry Road, watercolour by A. Perigal. St Cuthbert's Poorhouse (on the site of the Western General Hospital) is on the left of the picture.*

1O DOWNING STREET
LONDON SW1A 2AA

THE PRIME MINISTER

Any nation neglects the education of its young people at its peril, and the history of a great school like Fettes needs writing to set today's picture in perspective. The story of how each generation battled with its particular challenges carries the message of how the essential principles of modern education in state and private sector alike evolved. The story of Fettes is also a stirring tale in its own right. With its splendid setting in the great capital city of Scotland, Fettes has seen many changes in its 130-year history, and its story is the story of some remarkable individuals. The values which have characterised it over the years go back to the figure of Alexander Potts, first headmaster. His humanity, his powerful sense of duty and his inspirational teaching shaped a tradition that has been carried on in a remarkable way. As we approach the millennium, I hope that the boys and girls of Fettes reading this history will be proud of their school and carry into the future the torch of liberal values, duty and open-mindedness first lit back in 1870.

Tony Blair

November 1998

This book is dedicated to
all Fettesians
past and present.

Acknowledgements

So many Fettes people have shared their reminiscences and thoughts about the School with me that there is sadly no space to name them all, but to them all go my warmest thanks. The benign guiding presence behind this book is perhaps Freddy Macdonald, who taught at Fettes for 37 years and did so much to preserve a record of Fettes past. I am grateful to the Governing Body of the School for giving me the opportunity to write this book, and especially to Dame Mary Corsar for her unfailing support and advice. I also acknowledge the generous support of the Old Fettesian Association. Eric and Poppy Anderson, David Pighills, Francis Pearson, Bob Roberts, Susan and Jane McIntosh, Mark Peel, Andrew Murray, David Rhodes, Kate Eveling, Cameron Cochrane and Malcolm Thyne have all read sections of the text, and their advice has been warmly appreciated. I am grateful to Andrew Murray, Ralph Hughes and Peter Clarke for all their help with illustrations, and to Alastair Reid for his groundwork research into past Fettes staff and events. Finally my special thanks are due to Alexia Lindsay, the indefatigable Fettes archivist, whose enthusiasm and unrelenting pursuit of small but crucial facts brooked no obstacle.

Contents

Watercolour by David Bryce of the proposed College, 1863.

1

The Beginnings
A Father's Tragedy

On 11th June 1815, a young advocate from Edinburgh lay dying in Berlin. In the December of 1814 he had set off on the Grand Tour of Europe, where peace seemed at last to have dawned over the weary continent, but as he and his friend went round the sights, the news came like a thunderbolt from a clear sky that Napoleon had broken out of Elba and arrived in the south of France. As Bonaparte thrust rapidly northwards, the tourists pressed calmly on through the turmoil towards Berlin. But William had contracted typhoid on the journey, and the message now reached his father in Edinburgh that his only son was dying. On 17th May Sir William Fettes engaged the yacht *Comet* for the passage from Leith to Hamburg, where it arrived safely on 22nd May. We must imagine, then, that young William's parents were at his bedside when he died one week before the battle of Waterloo. He was 27.

Sir William Fettes never really got over the death of the only son who would have inherited his fortune, but he buried his grief by plunging back into business. Born in 1750, he had started his working life at the age of 18 as a grocer. The business went from strength to strength, with occasional distractions, as when he sat on the jury which convicted Deacon Brodie. When in 1795 he was given the contract for provisioning the army camps in Scotland, his fortunes took off in tandem with the Napoleonic Wars. By the time of his son's death he was not only a rich man, but a highly respected public figure. He had been Master of the Merchant Company, and Lord Provost twice between 1800 and 1806. As Lord Provost in 1800 and 1801, when the food shortage had sparked riots in many places, he kept the peace in Edinburgh by providing soup kitchens and devising a new drainage system. In 1804 he was created a Baronet.

After passing on the grocery business in 1804, Sir William concentrated on banking interests and managing the portfolio of estates and properties he had built up. In 1807 he moved into a new house at the north-west corner of Charlotte Square (No. 13), then on the edge of open country. His next-door neighbour Lord Cockburn was to write 20 years later:

> How can I forget the glory of that scene, on the still nights in which . . . I have stood in Queen Street or the opening at the north-west corner of Charlotte Square, and

William Fettes Jnr, 1787–1815.

1

listened to the ceaseless rural corn-craiks nestling happily in the long grass.

From this viewpoint, where urban elegance and rural peace lay side by side, Sir William could look to the north-west over the Moray Estate and the Water of Leith down to the sweeping fields of the estate at Comely Bank he had bought in 1800 from Sir Philip Ainslie of Pilton, where in time to come the landscape was to be overshadowed by a great school.

In his later years, Sir William became a benefactor of many causes and a pillar of the establishment. He helped to raise the money needed to move the New Club from St Andrew Square to larger premises in Princes Street, and in 1826 was on the committee appointed by the banks to oversee the bankruptcy of Sir Walter Scott. His wife died three weeks before him, and young William's death 20 years earlier meant that no-one was sure who would be the beneficiaries of his considerable fortune. He even hinted to his sister-in-law just before his wife's death that he would be leaving it to a lunatic asylum. When he died on 27th May 1836, however, his will stated that after minor bequests

> the residue of my whole Estate should form an Endowment for the maintenance, education and outfit of young people whose parents have either died without leaving sufficient funds for that purpose, or who, from innocent misfortune during their lives, are unable to give suitable education to their children.

The trustees were told to 'purchase or feu a proper situation near Edinburgh and to erect thereon a building suitable to the purposes of the Endowment, which shall be called "The Fettes Endowment for the Education, Maintenance and Outfit of Young People."' The trust funds Sir William left came (after bequests to each Trustee of £1,000) to just over £166,000, and the question of why it took 30 years to start spending it needs attention.

Edinburgh was not short of charitable 'hospitals' (as they were called) for educating poor children, as rich citizens like George Heriot, George Watson and Daniel Stewart had (in the words of *The Torch* for 7th March 1846) 'inundated the northern metropolis with their charity.' Many, though, were beginning to doubt their value. These 'loveless residential institutions' (as Magnus Magnusson described them) had a dour, monastic atmosphere, producing children who were (as an Inspector later told the Endowed Schools Commission) dishonest, selfish and intellectually inert. By 25th April 1846, *The Torch* was giving its ideas about the Fettes legacy:

> It seems no very wide departure from the will of the testator, no grievous encroachment on his benevolent purposes, to alter the destination of this from an object which the good sense of the community considers injurious to one of which it highly approves. [Otherwise] the money will be spent . . . probably in building a palace for charity children, which the growing intelligence of the people will before many years compel its guardians to shut up.

Sir William Fettes' Trustees, Lord Wood, Lord Rutherford and Thomas Corrie (who had all been at the Bar with young William) were undecided. They were not keen to replicate the hospital model and they wanted to fill a real need, but, because

Sir William Fettes, 1750–1836.

A contemporary silhouette of the Fettes family. Sir William is sitting second from the right, Lady Fettes, his wife, is standing third from the left.

they were unsure where that need lay, they procrastinated, watching Sir William's properties grow in value and awaiting developments. £166,000 might not be enough for their purposes, and it was likely to appreciate in an active property market.

Real developments did not come until the 1860s. It was a decade of educational ferment. In the 18th and early 19th centuries, the 'great' English schools had been barbaric places, but by the 1840s the example of Thomas Arnold at Rugby had shown that it was possible for a boarding school to be a civilised community. Abuses were still rife, though, and the schools' complacency was shattered by a public outcry at the start of the decade. An article by Henry Reeve in *The Edinburgh Review* in 1861 concentrated on Eton, where in earlier days it had been said that 'the inmates of a workhouse or gaol are better fed and lodged than the scholars of Eton'. The article blew the cover of the Provost and Fellows, who had managed to divide among themselves over the previous 20 years the £127,000 which came from fines on renewal of leases. The management of the nine best-known schools came under such heavy attack that only the setting up of the Clarendon Commission could damp down the furore. The debate widened as the Taunton Commission of 1864 looked into 800 other schools, and even produced a visionary scheme to merge all endowments to set up a national educational system for all classes, paying what they could afford, with a proper examination and inspection system and a modern curriculum with plenty of science. But when the Bill, the Endowed Schools Act of 1869, came, it had been purged of all its radical content by committees full of public school men, and resulted merely in the setting up of a permanent Commission to regulate endowments and keep an eye on governing bodies. The schools meanwhile had closed ranks and formed the Headmasters' Conference to resist inroads into their independence.

*Lord Inglis, Trustee of Fettes'
endowment trust, and first
Chairman of the Governors.*

The 1860s also saw a shift in the whole philosophy of English boarding education which was to influence the setting up of Sir William Fettes' school, as Arnold's ideal of 'godliness and good learning' gave way before the advance of manliness and good form. The muscular Christianity of the new age had been preached by men like F. D. Maurice and Charles Kingsley, author of *The Water Babies*. Kingsley believed the middle classes had become effeminate because their education did not contain enough of the experience of pain and endurance needed to bring out the masculine qualities. This Spartan ideal comes through in his enthusiasm for what was to become an institution at Sir William's school, the cold bath:

> That morning cold bath, which foreigners regard as young England's strangest superstition, has done as much to abolish drunken-ness as any other cause whatsoever. With a clean skin in healthy action, and nerves and muscles braced by a sudden shock, men do not crave for artificial stimulants.

The theory that physical discomfort was good for you harmonised with the unease some rich Victorian parents felt about bringing their children up in luxury. If their sons had to live so comfortably in the holidays, it would do them good to use term-time to appreciate that life has its tougher side. By the 1860s, this generalized feeling was sharpened by the vogue for team games involving physical contact. The fashion arose at schools like Marlborough, where George Cotton arrived in 1852. In November of the previous year his predecessor Matthew Wilkinson had had to cope with the last of the great school rebellions, involving gunpowder and disorder which raged for a week. Cotton quickly saw the need to channel the boys' taste for anarchy and afternoons spent annoying the Wiltshire farmers and killing rabbits and squirrels. He instituted team games. They canalised the aggression and filled in the afternoons which were all too available for misuse. Organised games began, therefore, as an instrument of social control, but soon headmasters in many schools were preaching the moral beauty of athleticism and team spirit. Once started, the games band-wagon rolled on unchecked.

In this decade of upheaval, the plans of Sir William Fettes' trustees at long last started to crystallise. For 24 years they had waited for the right blueprint for the new School. By 1857 Lord Rutherford had died, and three new trustees were appointed: Lord Inglis of Glencorse, the Hon. Bouverie Francis Primrose and Hugh Corrie, banker. Inglis, later to become the Lord Justice General, was a man with ideas. In 1859, the prospective school is still being called in the Trustees' Minutes 'an Hospital', in 1860 it is 'Fettes Institution', by 1861 'Fettes Endowment College' and by 1862 'Fettes College.' The Trustees' reluctance to create another 'hospital' exclusively for poor children was reinforced by the findings of the Argyll Commission, which considered the hospital system to be an evil, and the Act that followed the Commission in 1869 turned the hospitals at a stroke into fee-paying day schools for middle class parents of modest means. Numbers at schools like George Watson's instantly soared. But a completely new vision now floated before the eyes of the Fettes Trustees. The English public school system was finally cleaning up its act under pressure from Clarendon and Taunton. With the rapid growth of the middle classes and the spread of railways and evangelical religion, boarding public schools were proliferating. Boys from Scotland, even, were starting to travel south to attend them. This, thought the Trustees, was where the need lay in Edinburgh.

Edinburgh's golden age between 1820 and 1835 had brought new schools in the shape of the Edinburgh Academy, Merchiston Castle and (at Musselburgh) Loretto, but the Academy was a day school and Loretto was a preparatory school until it was bought by H. H. Almond in 1862. Merchiston was a small private school until it expanded in 1863, while up in Perthshire, Trinity College, Glenalmond, had been started in 1847 to instil the principles of the Anglican faith. The Fettes Trustees now decided that the professional classes were under-catered for, and arrived at the concept of 'a public school with a charitable foundation as its basis, but with a large superstructure of education and pupils, in which there is nothing either of gratuity or charity.' By 1864, it was being planned as a school with 50 boarders (the 'Foundationers', orphans or sons of needy parents) educated free from the endowment, and a further 50 (or more) day-boys paying fees. This then changed further as the School's distance from the city centre was increasingly seen as an obstacle to the success of day education, until in 1868 the decision was taken to erect further boarding houses and make it a fully boarding school, with no limit on the number of non-Foundationers.

Not everyone agreed, though, that this was what Sir William had wanted, and that it was right to use the endowment to build boarding houses for fee-paying (i.e. non-impoverished) pupils. The issue was to plague the Trustees, as would the perception that they were importing into Scotland a strictly English model, for many citizens of Edinburgh saw little in the English system that deserved copying. When the Argyll Commission surveyed Scottish schools in 1864–68, it found that in Scotland one child in 250 had some sort of higher education. The figure in England was one in 1,300. There was a school in nearly every parish, and science education in Scotland was as good as any in Europe. But while the Scottish educational tradition had great strengths, the Trustees argued that the public school system was transforming itself in the new age of accountability and that there was clear evidence of demand. The School would be following Sir William's wishes in educating 50 needy boys for free, but would make sure that, instead of being isolated 'charity children', they would be part of a dynamic community.

The Trustees had asked William Playfair, the key architect of the 'Athens of the North', to design their new school. His appointment gave promise of a neo-classical building, but when Playfair died in 1857, they appointed David Bryce, Playfair's arch-rival (whom in 1840 he had black-balled from the Architectural Institute of Scotland), and champion of every style from the Baronial to the Baroque. Bryce, designer of many Edinburgh banks, the Royal Infirmary and around 150 country houses, was a very different prospect from Playfair. To choose him was to choose intricacy, flamboyance, prodigality. He built to be noticed, and the site offered him by the Trustees was wonderfully conspicuous, dominating the north-western vista from the New Town. The ridge at the top of the long rise northward from Comely Bank commanded a magnificent view of the city, rising to the skyline framed by

David Bryce, Architect of Fettes College. Oil painting by John Zephaniah Bell.

The laying of the foundation stone of Fettes College.

the Pentland Hills on the west and Arthur's seat on the east, and punctuated by Edinburgh Castle, St Giles' Cathedral and the great tenements of the Old Town. 'There is no situation round Edinburgh so suitable,' Bryce told the Trustees on 5th January 1860. Synthesising the Scottish Baronial style with the French Gothic of the Loire valley, he created his masterpiece on this site. It was to be a unique and astonishing building, but the extravagance of the external ornament, the gargoyles, the bartizans, the gilded ironwork and the crockets and pinnacles of the traceried gablets, helped to drain the Fettes coffers. The original legacy of £166,000 had risen by now to £484,000, and in 1864 the Trustees were predicting that the main building would cost £80,000. They reckoned without Bryce's ambitions. It was to cost nearly £140,000 (with another £15,000 for the sick-house, gym, lodges, gates, railings and roads) – a share of the endowment which, when added to the high salary levels fixed by the Trustees, was in the end to leave too little for the future needs of the School and its pupils. If Playfair had lived and produced a classical design it would have saved the stone-masons infinite pains and cost far less, though it would have been much less distinctive in the 'Athens of the North'. The Fettes building remains a remarkable monument to Victorian taste. It has had its detractors, such as George Scott Moncreiff, describing it in 1947, at the high tide of modernism, as 'a monumental Victorian whatnot, a vast blight and blot looming over a wide area of low country.' But the wheel of taste turns. The eclecticism of Bryce's château delights the post-modernist, and by 1990 Charles McKean was able to describe it as 'undeniably one of Scotland's greatest buildings.'

On 25th June 1864 the foundation stone was laid for the new School by the

6

Honourable Frederica Primrose, wife of one of the Trustees, with a short speech. 'While Scotland can boast of excellent and celebrated schools,' she declared, 'there are none which can be said to bear exactly the stamp and character which will attach to this College. It will take its place amongst those seats of learning which have stood highest in the world's history, and add new names to that array of men of genius, knowledge and science for which the ancient capital of Scotland has been so long distinguished.'

The School was to open in 1870. It had all taken time, but the vision of the founder was at last ready to be realised. Sir William had seen the gift of knowledge as something beyond price, as he wrote in his account book:

> Study is not a toil but a recreation to the great. It prepares the mind for the encountering of dangers, it relieves us from many a pang which prejudice had inflicted. It teaches us the means of happiness. It fills up in an interesting manner the vacuity of leisure. It impresses us with serious and useful truths. It is a treasure that repays us for all misfortunes, and it renders us not only happy in ourselves, but also the pleasing companions of others.

The vision of bringing it to the children of others had emerged from the death of his own son. 'It is a moving thought,' David MacMyn was to say at Founder's Day in 1958, 'that from a father's tragedy there emerged a creation far beyond his dreams, which has given priceless benefit to later generations of young men.'

The Lead Bee from the Chapel roof, part of Sir William's insignia and part of the School's coat of arms. The School's motto Industria *derives from the 'busy' bee.*

The School in its first year, July 1871.

2

The Only Thing Worth Living For
POTTS : 1870–89

'The entrance hall itself was strewn with heaps of rubbish, from which we gazed up through the scaffolding at the place where the bells were to be. Ladders and shavings were common in the corridors, and the smell of paint and varnish blended curiously with our strange weird feelings, which still wandered with wonder between the present before us and the past we had left.' The boys who anxiously explored the unfinished School on 5th October 1870 were later to be called the Patriarchs. That warm, sunny afternoon they were a group of 53 bewildered 9–14-year-olds starting on a new and forbidding adventure. Six of them – the top performers in the Scholarship examination – had come the day before to be inspired with a privileged vision of the School's future. The rest had travelled that day from Edinburgh in cabs bumping up the narrow, muddy country lane, full of ruts and big stones, which ran up to the College from the east corner of Comely Bank. It was only when they were summoned to the Dining Hall for tea that they finally encountered the Presence. The Presence was that of Alexander William Potts, the first and perhaps the greatest of the Headmasters of Fettes. 'He came into Hall, gave us a welcome and shook hands with everyone,' recalled John Parsons. 'His dignity – I had almost said majesty – and his beautiful voice, impressed my small mind then, and I have never lost the impression.'

Potts' career to date had been distinguished enough. Born in 1834, the son of a Birmingham businessman, he went to school at Shrewsbury, where he became captain of football and boats and Second Head of School. There he picked up his passion for the Classics from its eminent Headmaster, Benjamin Hall Kennedy, author of the famous Latin Primer and the greatest teacher of his age. This formidable character once expelled the whole of the Sixth Form for grammatical inaccuracies (though he let them come back the next day). At Shrewsbury, wrote Henry Nevinson, 'the School breathed Greek. To enter Headroom was to become a scholar . . . Winged iambics fluttered through the air; they hung like bats on the shelves, and the dust fell in Greek particles.' This inspirational schooling helped Potts win a Scholarship to St John's College, Cambridge, where he won the second First of his year and the Junior Chancellor's Medal, before having a taste of teaching in a temporary post at Charterhouse. He then went back to St John's as a Fellow for

Alexander William Potts, aged 19, while still at Shrewsbury School. Original drawing by Herbert M. Luckock, 1853.

9

three years, before making a crucial move in 1862. He was offered a post at Rugby, and so entered there the post-Arnold *milieu* which was the breeding ground for so many Victorian Headmasters.

Thomas Arnold had died in 1842, but the torch of 'godliness and good learning' he had lit still shone brightly. The father figure pictured by Thomas Hughes in *Tom Brown's Schooldays* had changed the direction of 19th-century education. The way he applied his Christian faith to school life was crucial in ending the barbarism of school boarding life in the 18th and the first quarter of the 19th century. He made war on vice: 'That ashy paleness and that awful frown were almost always the expression of deep ineffable scorn and indignation at the sight of vice and sin,' wrote his biographer Stanley. His School became a breeding ground for idealistic and talented schoolmasters. The degree to which Potts embraced the Rugby method is illustrated by his 'Commonplace Book'. This book, in which he kept 246 'scraps', starts with a solemn series of twelve *Arnoldiana* (pronouncements of the great man). The systems laid down at Rugby for training character and giving authority to senior boys imprinted themselves on his mind as a model. Nor was he alone. Schoolmasters who had served under Arnold or lived in his aftermath went forth to colonise the British public schools – Cotton and Bradley to Marlborough, Benson to Wellington, Percival to Clifton, Hart to Sedbergh, Vaughan to Harrow, Philpotts to Bedford, Butler to Haileybury and Prince Lee to King Edward's, Birmingham. When he took the Arnold gospel to a school in Scotland, Potts may

The college being built, c.*1869.*

*Cottages which were later
removed from the Fettes estate.*

have given up a prominent niche in the hall of fame of English education, but in
retrospect must rank among the greatest of all Victorian Headmasters.

Potts transplanted to Fettes Arnold's system of prefects and fagging. Before
Arnold, prefects had usually been tyrants, but he turned them into a character-
forming elite. 'The Doctor' was not above simply expelling unsuitable boys from
Rugby, to make sure that the ones who survived to the Sixth Form shared his value-
system. 'The first, second and third duty of a schoolmaster,' he wrote, 'is to get rid
of unpromising subjects.' The ethos was crucial. The point of education was to turn
out Christian gentlemen. To keep at school big older boys who might be good at
games but were not clever and might be bullies did not give a good moral example
to the younger ones. He hoped to sieve out the philistine, boorish elements, leaving as prefects those who identified with him and would provide a moral lead. This
was all very well, but not all headmasters were as effective or ruthless as Arnold in
establishing a high moral tone in the Sixth Form. Maybe they had more of a need
to keep numbers up. The form in which the prefect system pervaded the public
schools of the land was a tremendous improvement on what had preceded it, but
always potentially flawed in practice. Potts, however, was happy to accept Arnold's
view, that 'a Public School cannot be governed other than by Prefects.'

Potts rapidly won respect as Sixth Form Master at Rugby, where he married
Ellen Bowden Smith, who had been brought up in the New Forest and on the
Continent and had a social conscience to match his own. One odd episode at the
end of his time there suggests that his tact and diplomacy were highly valued. After
Potts' appointment to Fettes (in 1868), the headship fell vacant at Rugby itself.
Henry Hayman, Headmaster of Bradfield, was appointed, but the staff almost to a
man disagreed with the choice. Hayman was admittedly a slightly pompous man,
who instead of 'Put out the light!' would say 'Adumbrate the scintillation!', but
much of the feeling was sheer prejudice. In a bizarre move Potts was dispatched to

Bradfield to tell him he would not be welcome at Rugby. His persuasive powers were not equal to the task. Hayman persisted in taking up the post, only to be hounded out within four years.

Amongst Potts' rivals for the Headmastership of Fettes was Frederick Farrar, author of the sentimental school classic *Eric, or Little by Little* and soon to be Master of Marlborough and later Dean of Canterbury. He was an advocate of science in the curriculum, and the history of the School would have been very different if he had been appointed. In the end, however, there was no real contest. Potts presented 23 testimonials to support his application. They were irresistible. Dr Temple of Rugby referred to 'the extreme reluctance with which I contemplate the possibility of his departure,' and Dr Kennedy, his teacher at Shrewsbury and now Professor of Greek at Cambridge, wrote: 'I never met with any boy whose work showed more energy of purpose and execution . . . I consider him indeed a man of remarkable power, great decision and, I believe, great tact and judgement in dealing with boys; I need hardly add, a man of high principle, of enlarged and progressive views, not at all disposed to lag in the rear of modern advancement.' Again and again, the testimonials stressed his kindness and his progressive outlook. He was appointed to take up office in 1870. His Rugby friend and colleague Clem Cotterill shared his pioneering spirit and interest in social reform. It was decided that he would join Potts to carry their shared brand of mild Christian socialism to the new Scottish school. Cotterill later recalled their discussion at Rugby:

> We had much talk of the subject, and one evening we left his house and he saw me home to mine. When it was all arranged that I should come, we still stood talking at

Clem Cotterill (seated third from the left) with boys. Stewart Ponsonby, Captain of football, stands second from the right.

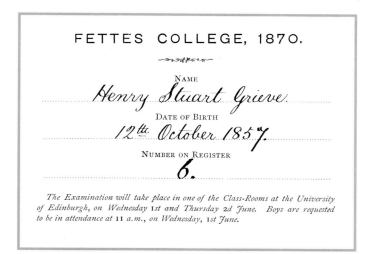

FETTES COLLEGE, 1870.

NAME

Henry Stuart Grieve.

DATE OF BIRTH

12ᵗʰ October 1857.

NUMBER ON REGISTER

6.

The Examination will take place in one of the Class-Rooms at the University of Edinburgh, on Wednesday 1st and Thursday 2d June. Boys are requested to be in attendance at 11 a.m., on Wednesday, 1st June.

A ticket for the first entrance exam.

the door; then suddenly he stretched out his hand and grasped mine with these words, "Now with the help of God the place shall move on."

It is a touching picture of shared hopes, and of the Christian ideal with which Potts approached his task.

He planned carefully in advance, laying out his ideas for the detailed organisation of the new School in two long letters to the Trustees. Food, fees and chaplaincy were three subjects on which he felt strongly. He was quite definite that the boys should be fed centrally. This was most unusual, but Potts had seen how at Rugby the housemasters could not resist the temptation to make money by feeding their boys cheaply. It took another century for this to become (more or less) universal practice. Bunny Seaton, who had been Temple's butler at Rugby, was appointed Fettes Steward, a post he occupied for 35 years.

As for fees, Potts wanted them never to be raised. 'It is always an unpleasant thing to raise the fees. Parents who have contemplated sending their sons are with difficulty persuaded that no wrong is being done to them.' This delightful notion, which would sound a sympathetic chord in the hearts of parents of every generation, did not sound one with the Trustees, and they also adjusted Potts' recommended fee level (£20) upwards to £25 (still cheaper than most rival schools; at Rugby they were £40). On the Chaplaincy, Potts felt even more strongly. He was very devout, and the spiritual well-being of his boys was close to his heart, but he did not see an actual chaplaincy as the right instrument for ensuring this. A chaplain has to be chosen from a denomination, and Potts' ideal was non-denominational Christianity. The views he expressed to the Trustees were deeply felt:

> If a really national church be possible, and such a possibility may still be not beyond hope, it will be possible when Christians come to see that the points on which they are at one are infinitely more important than the differences which separate them into sects. To bring our pupils to see that while they retain the differences of cult which are the natural offspring of the accidents of their birth they still belong in a wide sense to a family and that they can unite in the common worship of a common Father

13

under the guidance of their ordinary teachers will be to impart to them a lesson which in after life they will find of far greater value than the most precise and minute acquaintance with the finer subtleties of their distinctive creeds.

All the teachers were, in a sense, to be chaplains.

I should therefore regard the appointment of a Chaplain as a most serious evil and a great blow to the influence which I wish the Masters to exercise.

The Trustees accepted these progressive views, though aware that they could be misunderstood. Potts was most unusual for a headmaster of his time in not being ordained, and to have no cleric on the staff was likely to seem odd. In the summer term of 1871 Fettes had a visit from Thomas Huxley, humanist and champion of Darwinian evolution. A glance at the staff list showed Huxley that not one of them was in Orders. He congratulated Potts on such an enlightened set of appointments, and advised him to go on steering clear of clergy. Potts passed the story on a month later to his next visitor, Benjamin Jowett, the distinguished Master of Balliol. 'So like dear Huxley,' growled Jowett. 'He is narrow-minded enough to be in Orders himself.'

The School community that assembled for the first time in the Call-over Hall at 5 p.m. on 5th October 1870 consisted of 53 boys and seven masters. The boys formed a talented group. Two were to become Major-Generals, one Physician to the King, one a Bishop; one was to play rugby for Scotland and one was to win the Porson Prize. They were divided that year into School House (42 non-fee-paying 'Foundationers' under Alexander Bell and J. A. Blaikie), and Moredun House, then called Glencorse (11 fee-paying boarders under Clem Cotterill). Clem Cotterill, Housemaster of Glencorse for 20 years, was Potts' friend and Deputy. His views were 'daring, not to say revolutionary. He was by no means a crank, but a genuine idealist of the William Morris breed.' He believed (as his later book *Suggested Reforms in Public Schools* revealed) that competitive examinations were bad and that class distinctions should be abolished by ensuring in school a cross-section of all classes. Cotterill was later to be a candidate for the headmastership on Potts' death, but the trouble was, he was slightly eccentric and not enough of a disciplinarian. 'His lectures to the House on matters of discipline often struck a note that verged on the ridiculous,' wrote Alfred Hamilton Grant. Then there was his sniff, caused either by chronic catarrh or 'super-sensitive olfactory nerves which led him to suspect bad smells with all and sundry.' But he was a fine housemaster, an enthusiast who championed his boys through thick and thin and was loved by them in return.

After a few days to settle in, work began on Monday 10th October at 7.30 a.m. After a test, the boys were put in three forms. Their diet was Classics above all (though, as in the great English schools, this subject included history, divinity and English) and three of the five staff were classicists (Potts, Cotterill and Bell). Maths was taught by Blaikie, modern languages by H. E. Goldschmidt. Potts had appointed a modern linguist with some hesitation. Not everyone was agreed that modern languages was a proper subject, and its exponents had a reputation for not being able to keep order. There was no worry on that score with 'Froggy' Goldschmidt. He kept control with a little black ruler and 'sudden descents from his dais upon

A. W. Potts.

boys who had been exceptionally careless or stupid, and grabbing of their books, pen, pencil and paper. These would all be hurled out of the classroom window.' It seemed to work. Music was covered by Joseph (Joey) Geoghegan, and A. (Huxty) Huxtable, organist and piano teacher.

Football (rugby) was begun on 12th October, with a massive game involving the entire School (apart from one delicate boy) and three masters. Each side had five backs and 22 or 23 forwards. The ball was round, and further disorder was caused by the fact that only two boys knew the rules, and that (as referees had not yet been invented) any disputed point had to be argued out by the two captains. Other players tended to join in, and the disputes could last up to a quarter of an hour. The game of rugby football, then in its infancy, was to be one of the keys to the rapid fame of the new School. Potts, who used to practise place-kicks with the boys, was in favour, provided games-players always observed the highest standards. In a speech at an Edinburgh dinner, he declared: 'I should like my boys and all boys, and all men, to be ever mindful, in the hottest scrimmage and in the most exciting period of the game, that they are not only football players but Christians and gentlemen.' The greatest champion of exercise, though, was Cotterill. He was bothered by the thought of boys killing time in the afternoons, and believed, as he said in his book *Suggested Reforms in Public Schools*, that the mere scholar was half man, half ghost. The mere athlete was in his turn half man, half beast, and Cotterill wanted neither ghosts nor beasts at Fettes, so after a morning in the classroom the boys should be out in the open air. 'The keen wind,' he wrote, 'serves but to brace and harden them; to clear their brains and sweeten their tempers; to purify not only the blood, but surely to help, in so far as we can be helped by such agencies, to purify also their hearts.' He made friends with the aerobically-minded Hely Hutchison Almond, Headmaster of Loretto School in Musselburgh. When Almond visited Fettes to preach, he used to jog the seven miles from Musselburgh, though wisely accompanied by his carriage in case the exertion proved too great. He played himself in the Loretto cricket XI until he was 48; no objections from rival teams are recorded. Such was his passion for team games that he was even said to eat his handkerchief when his side was losing, and in later years had to be restrained 'by force' from going to watch rugby matches, as it was bad for his heart. Cotterill and Almond formed a partnership to develop the team-game element in the public schools which was later to result in the Fettesian-Lorettonian Club, and influence the development of the game of rugby itself.

Within a fortnight in that first term a second game was started, and the sides reduced to the normal size of 20. The next thing was to fix up a match to inject the flavour of competition. The result was not a success: 'Today we went to play Scott's School.' wrote John Parsons in his diary. 'It was a dirty game. We won, but they said we didn't, so we came away.' Poppy Anderson has suggested that Scott's School was the Edinburgh Academy, of which Sir Walter Scott was the best-known founding Trustee. J. Darling dropped a goal, or so the Fettes team thought. The opposition said it was punted and, with no referee, the argument that followed became so heated that even Cotterill and Blaikie, who were watching, took off their coats and

Henry Goldschmidt.

15

joined in. It was a 'very sanguinary encounter,' but no decision was reached, 'so we came away.'

That first winter of 1870–71 was a hard one. 'There was black frost from the middle of December to the end of January, and then there was deep snow.' Living was spartan for the Patriarchs. 'In the new unfinished College the cold was bitter; there was no central heating in those days, and few fires.' In this chilly environment, the Fettesian would get up at 7 a.m. and have a cold bath in the shallow, flat-bottomed bath in his cubicle. If the water was iced over, he could break it with a hair-brush. If there was time, he dusted out his study and cleaned out the fire. This had to be quick, as the first lesson was at 7.30 a.m. It was followed by Chapel at 8.45 a.m. and then breakfast (porridge or a tiny slice of cold meat with bread and butter). School then went on until lunch-time (meat and either soup, pudding or fish). It was then games until just before 4 p.m., followed by a rush to the changing-rooms to wash off the mud in cold water (hot water for prefects only) in time for afternoon school. This went on for two or two and a half hours until tea (bread and 'not quite enough' butter; jam at the weekends), followed by prep, supper (porridge, or bread and cheese with beer), prayers and, at 9.30 p.m., bed (before which 'it is hoped that no boy will fail to avail himself of this opportunity for Private Prayer'). At least the sanitation was good. Potts had perhaps learnt from his own schooling at Shrewsbury, where Kennedy the Headmaster once reported to a worried Inspector that he had doubled the number of lavatories in his boarding house. There were now two. The food provided by Steward 'Bunny' Seaton proved adequate to raise generations of powerful rugby players, but lacked finesse. Bunny's blonde daughter won more admiration from the boys than his menus.

In the classroom, Classics reigned supreme, with maths and languages very much a side-show. Science was notably absent, in keeping with Arnold's view that it was likely to divert pupils' minds from 'more important matters'. Being a strong academic, Potts aimed from the start to drive the School towards the highest goals of scholarship. The Classics were to dominate the curriculum for the first 75 years of the School's life. The excellence of the teaching and the impact of Fettes scholarship at Oxford and Cambridge were the mainspring of the School's astonishing early success. The supremacy of Latin and Greek was sustained by Oxford and Cambridge Universities, where science was still thought vulgar. The Classics were the key to upward mobility, and there was a good deal of snobbery involved, seen in its most extreme form in the words of Thomas Gaisford, Professor of Greek at Oxford earlier in the century: 'The advantages of a classical education are twofold. It enables us to look down with contempt on those who have not shared its advantages, and also fits us for places of emolument not only in this world but also in that which is to come.' Potts, however, was the least snobbish of men, and taught the Classics because he loved them, and actually believed that to study them made you better. In his commonplace book he quotes from Plato, *Philebus 16*: 'The ancients were better than us. They lived nearer the gods.' The unchanging precision of the rules of grammar called forth the virtue of persistence. As a boy hacked his way through the jungle of gerunds or struggled through the quicksands of *Oratio*

The interior of an early dormitory. Drawing by A. S. Hartrick.

Alexander William Potts, Headmaster 1870–89.

William Augustus Heard, Headmaster 1890–1919.

The College from the south-west: watercolour by J. W. Parsons.

The Sixth Form Room, drawing by A. S. Hartrick (School House, 1877).

Obliqua, he was showing the very fibre that would fit him to go forth and help run the Empire or serve his fellow-man. As a teacher, Potts had the gift of inspiring the youthful mind – unlike all too many of his contemporaries. Schoolmasters often saw the ancient authors as quarries from which to hack out grammatical forms or intriguing bits of syntax. 'This term,' said one Victorian headmaster to his class, 'you are to have the privilege of reading the *Oedipus Coloneus* of Sophocles, a veritable treasure-house of grammatical peculiarities.' Not so Potts. Henry Hamilton Fyfe was to remember that 'Reading the *Republic* or Cicero's *De Natura Deorum* with the Head was like having windows opened on to eternal oceans of speculation, eternal mountain ranges of earnest thought.'

For Potts was, wrote Parsons, 'a man whose very presence served as inspiration, even to smudgy-faced little boys, doing their best to avoid learning anything . . . He was magnificently handsome in the ancient Greek style . . . His voice had music in it. His walk was majestic.' 'The swing of his silk gown,' Fyfe recalled, 'as he strode down the corridor to the Sixth Form Room was one of indefinable majesty . . . a great calm, broad brow, the most wonderful violet eyes, full of truth and steadfastness, and poetry and kindliness.' He had, so the story went, been asked by Sir Noel Paton to sit for a picture of Christ. Cotterill was later to speak of 'the atmosphere of general glow which encircled him and emanated from him.' To sit with him in the Sixth Form Room and read the classical authors was to breathe a special air, to glimpse, suddenly, new possibilities in yourself. So it happened that within

17

Above: *a College reading room;* above right: *a College study. Both drawings by J. W. Parsons (School House, 1870).*

A memorandum for house masters, 17th March 1886.

Fettes College.

MEMORANDUM FOR HOUSE-MASTERS AND FORM-MASTERS.

Things which should be attended to every Term.

THE attention of a Master may frequently be turned by circumstances in some special direction, and in consequence he may forget how long a time has elapsed since he impressed upon his boys the importance of some things indispensable to a healthy school life. The following hints are intended to remind Masters of matters which should be brought before those for whom they are responsible, perhaps each Term. This is not to be done mechanically, or simultaneously, or necessarily at the beginning of Term. Each Master must judge for himself as to when and how, ἐξαγοραζόμενος τὸν καιρόν.

Each Form-Master should speak to his boys about—

Copying; use of cribs; honesty of work; punctuality; neatness; respect for property; the duty of not defacing the building, or injuring desks; responding in chapel.

A House-Master should feel it a duty boldly to face the moral problem, and to speak about the temptations which a boy may meet with at school.

To the House he should speak about the imperative necessity of observing the Cubicle Rule; the value, intellectually and morally, of bodily exercise; of the virtue of manliness and self-restraint; of neighbourly conduct towards outsiders, with especial reference to snow-balling; of temperance in eating and drinking; of avoiding dirty talk and low literature; of avoiding betting and gambling in all forms. Attention should also be called to clothing, precautions against colds, wearing of greatcoats while watching matches in winter, the danger of lying on damp grass in spring and summer, and wearing of caps.

The things which a Form-Master should bring before his boys would also naturally from time to time be brought by a House-Master before the House as a whole.

A. W. P.

17th March 1886.

the new Scottish school the unmistakable signs of true scholarship were emerging. The high point of the process was Greek and Latin composition, as *Samson Agonistes* might be put into iambics, or Prescott into Greek prose in the style of Thucydides. Incredible pains were taken over these esoteric tasks, and the best of all were put into 'The Book' and kept in the School Library for all to admire.

As that first year passed, the School settled into a routine. Discipline was not a serious problem in a small, young school, but the right sanctions had to be identified. The hope was that, with the day's routine crammed full of activity, the boys would not have enough time to get into trouble. Although there was corporal punishment, it was in a mild form compared to other public schools of the day, and many offences were simply punished by attendance at a regular punishment drill. Names and misdemeanours were entered in the Drill Book, and a copy which still survives lists with charming pedantry offences which are predictably adolescent. Boys are put in for 'gross obliviousness', 'untimely pugnacity', 'ignorance of the use of the domestic pocket handkerchief', 'inclination to gambol', 'bringing a dog into the music room' or 'fooling with a razor'. Macfarlane 'indulged in untimely rejoicings', while MacLeod 'made imprudent use of an elastic catapult'. Being 'pugilistic', 'loquacious', 'shooing and pert' or 'undressed in Preparation' were also thought to justify punishment drill. In the boarding houses, bullying was dealt with by 'gymshoeing'. The whole house lined up in order of seniority to strike the offender with a gymshoe. This undignified punishment, alarmingly primitive as it seems, was designed to bring home to the bully a sense that his bullying was condemned by the entire community. Housemasters were supposed to pre-empt sexual offences by a well-timed homily. They should, Potts told them in their conditions of service, 'feel it a duty to face the moral problem, and to speak about the temptations which a boy may meet with at school.' How well this was done one can only imagine. The delicacy of Potts' own way of dealing with breaches of etiquette can be seen in his treatment of a Sixth Form boy who appeared in a light-coloured suit. Nothing was said at the time, but when Potts met him later out of doors, he took his arm and walked round with him for a time. Then he said: 'That's a very nice suit of yours, C. If I were going out to catch a salmon, I should like to have such a suit myself; but I am not sure that it is the best colour for reading Homer in.'

As the grim winter of 1870–71 gave way to spring, spirits rose and the games programme expanded. Hockey, athletics and cricket were begun, though a static game like cricket was not always suited to the School's micro-climate, when the unrelenting west wind howled down the main 'Below field' or the *haar* drifted in off the Forth. A professional called Humphrey was hired, however, and coached the boys well until a trip to Glasgow, from which he returned 'much the worse for wear'. His successor was called Beardsall, a Nottingham man, though unfortunately he 'could neither bowl nor bat', which didn't help. When he sent up a wide to the off, a favourite ball of his, he would shout 'Coot that, sir. Them's fine balls to coot.' Things settled down when Tom Sellars was appointed, but as time passed, cricket seemed continually under threat as the summer game from 'that canker-worm lawn tennis'.

The summer of 1871 saw the first Founder's Day, with speeches in the Upper. This included the 'Vive-La', a verse chronicle of the School's year sung by the Head of School which has been a unique ingredient of the Day ever since, in spite of its notoriously bad rhymes. The School was already making a highly favourable impact

The cricket team, 1885.

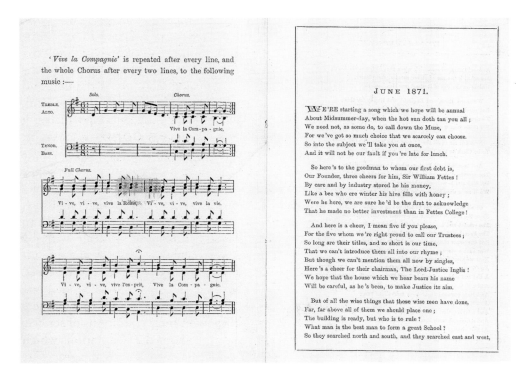

Excerpt from the first 'Vive-La', 1871.

on visitors. A father who saw round in April 1871 wrote to his wife: 'I think I have found just the school for Jack. I have seen nothing like it anywhere else, and I am very much pleased with the masters. It is a place called Fettes College . . . The building is a splendid one. But handsome as it is, nothing can be more sensible or appropriate than the internal fitting and arrangements. It is impossible to imagine anything better for its purpose. I will tell you some details of the arrangements for dormitories, lavatories, meals, hospital, recreation etc. when we meet. It would take too long to write. The fees are moderate – about £100 a year clears all. The feeding is liberal and abundant, and all the domestic arrangements little short of perfection. I have never seen anything like it.' Luckily for Fettes and for Jack Wills, he came. He ended up as Head of School, won the School's first Scholarship, at Balliol, Oxford, and set a mile record which lasted for 63 years. Few prospective parents could fail to be impressed by Potts. On 8th October 1871, he had a visit from no less a person than the Prime Minister, Mr. Gladstone. 'Went with the Lord Advocate to see the Fettes College,' Gladstone confided to his diary. 'Much pleased with Mr Potts.' Gladstone was taken with the plain life-style of the boys as a basis for the intellectual life. Ten months later, Queen Victoria noticed the School from the Queensferry Road, as she noted in her Journal for 16th August.

Numbers rose sharply to 95 for the year 1871–72, and to 137 for the following year. The income from the Fettes Trust was able to keep 48 Foundationers ('children of necessitous families'), but the number of paying boarders responded to demand, and had risen from 16 in the first year to 89. The School's reputation was spreading fast. The boys entering the School nearly all came straight from home

The gymnasium at the turn of the century.

20

(governesses or private tutors) until Potts' friend Charles Darnell followed him north in 1872 to start Cargilfield School in Trinity, Edinburgh. As the building programme neared completion, the gymnasium and chapel were ready for Easter 1872, and by the summer Carrington House (named, like the other 'out-houses', after the estate of one of the Trustees) was opened. Bell was moved from School House into Carrington as its first Housemaster, to be replaced by a new appointment, W. A. Heard, who was to follow him into Carrington when he left in 1875, and later become Headmaster. Carrington was first called Dalmeny, but its name was changed when Lord Rosebery, whose own house was called Dalmeny, complained that all his mail was going to Fettes. In 1873, Glencorse House was ready to take boys, and Cotterill moved there, taking the name with him from his old House, which was now renamed Moredun under Blaikie. Blaikie's successor in School House was W. P. Brooke, who ended up marrying Cotterill's sister and becoming the father of the poet Rupert Brooke.

The 'Patriarchs' were now ready to be given posts of authority. The records of three will never be equalled: William Lee held office as Head of School, G. C. Robertson as Captain of cricket and Stewart Ponsonby as Captain of football for five years each. The first prefects were appointed, but, embarrassingly, the appointments had to be held up for six weeks after six of the boys chosen were found smoking.

As numbers rose and the boys got older, the School's sporting reputation spread rapidly. By 1873, the cricket XI had found their feet. After beating the 2nd XIs of the Academy and Merchiston Castle by an innings each, they were allowed to play their 1st XIs, and won comfortably. The standard of football in particular was driven up rapidly by the commitment of Cotterill and other masters. They would join in the games on the main pitch (called Bigside after the pitch at Rugby), and John Parsons kept a handful of beard taken off one of the original masters in the scrum, which was later offered to the School museum. Cotterill stayed carefully clean-shaven. House matches were begun very soon (School House against the rest), and were played with total commitment, resembling 'a Homeric battle' where 'most of the warriors were wounded.'

There was a brief flirtation with the other brand of football as it grew in popularity, and, in order to be certain which code to follow, Fettes, in its third ever Association Football match, rather ambitiously took on Heart of Midlothian in 1878 (at home). Hearts won 8 - 2, but though this was not a disgrace, it was noticed that one of the Fettes goals was scored 'after a rugby-style charge.' Habits were not really going to change, and the die was cast for rugby. The game was itself changing fast, and Fettesians were destined to play a big part in this development. In 1871 the Headmaster of Loretto refereed the first ever game between Scotland and England at Raeburn Place near the School, steering Scotland to a narrow win with a disputed try. Asked about his umpiring principles, Almond declared: 'When an umpire is in doubt, I think he is justified in deciding against the side which makes the most noise. They are probably in the wrong.' In 1875, 15-a-side became the norm, though the ball was still round and tries had to be converted if they were to count.

The first proper season for Fettes against other schools was 1873–74, when all the matches were technically drawn as no tries were converted. The next year Fettes beat Loretto and Merchiston, and by 1876–7 were School Champions (in the terminology of the newspapers which followed school matches avidly), with even the Edinburgh Academy among the scalps. It was the start of a great run of success. The game then was virtually one continuous scrum, so a series of powerful packs helped Fettes. The player who got the ball ran until he was tackled and then lay on it until he was hacked off. It was a period of experiment in back play, and for the Academy match of 1878 Fettes adopted the lay-out of a full-back, two halves (called quarter-backs) and three three-quarters (called halves). This change made a crucial difference in encouraging passing of the ball, and Fettes can claim to have helped to pioneer an immensely influential change in the game. The 1879–80 XV was exceptional and was captained by the legendary A. R. Don Wauchope, know as 'Bunny'. Bunny and his team developed the art of passing with the aid of the new formation, and Loretto followed suit in the same year. As scrums could be interminable, the Fettes team invented 'hoicking' – sticking your leg into the scrum and hoicking the ball out for the backs to run with. Merchiston objected to all this and went on concentrating on the scrum. In their school magazine, a report on a defeat by Loretto contained the words: 'Our opponents passed the ball before they were held, tactics which we then thought somewhat unworthy.'

It was in 1880 that an effort was made to change the School colours (which up till then had been magenta and chocolate brown, racing colours of the Earl of Rosebery, father of Trustee Francis Primrose) into yellow and blue or black. Brown and magenta were certainly not everyone's cup of tea and when washed had tended to run into one another, but in ten years they had accumulated the sanctity of tradition, and anyway the new colours would make the players look like wasps. Three 'old fellows' wrote in from Ceylon, aghast at the proposal to 'change the dear old stripes that have been carried with glory through many an enemy's goal-posts.' The idea was rejected.

Below: *the XX of 1873–74; below right: the XV of 1875–6, captained by S. G. Ponsonby.*

22

EDINBURGH, FROM THE CASTLE, LOOKING NORTH. 4600. G

At Cambridge, Edgar Storey became the first Fettesian Blue in 1878 and captained the Cambridge XV in 1879. But the real cult-figure was Bunny Wauchope. 'Black-haired, nervy and dynamic,' he brought a new dimension to the running game. Captain of Cambridge by 1882, he started to attract crowds wherever he played. On tour in Huddersfield he drew from the crowd the cry 'E's like a bloomin' eel. They can't 'old 'im no'ow!' In 1881 the University put up a Cup for the old boys of rugby-playing schools. By now there were 21 Fettesians in residence (or 13 if we believe Robert Carruthers, which would mean that Fettes played two men short). In spite of this, the Fettes team won the Cup.

The infant Scottish school had arrived. Among the apostles of 'muscularity', its feats at Cambridge marked it out as a great nursery of rugby football. The classical dons at Oxford and Cambridge, meanwhile, started to rub their eyes at the quality of the scholarship emerging from it. The first Scholarship to Oxford won by Jack Wills in 1876 was followed by a string of others. In 1881 James Duff won the Porson Prize, the blue riband of Cambridge scholarship. The Prize had, up till then, been confined to the products of a few great English schools like Rugby and Shrewsbury, yet in the 1880s it was won no less than six times by a Fettesian. This astonishing record set the seal on the School's academic reputation. Faced by such

The view of Fettes College from Edinburgh Castle, 1874. Photograph by George Washington Wilson.

23

Alan Campbell Swinton.

The first page of Charles Henry Steel's first letter home, 1882.

feats, few could credit that the School had only opened in 1870.

The quality, above all, of Potts' teaching had within ten years projected his School into the academic front rank of British schools. He was meanwhile being pressed by his staff to broaden the curriculum from the classical monopoly, and give mathematics and modern languages more of a chance. He started a 'Modern School' in 1878. In November he reported to the Trustees: 'I admit personally that I share the views of the Bishop of Exeter in disliking bifurcation . . . I find myself in a minority . . . I hope to make a start with it after Christmas.' 'Bifurcation' was Potts' word for a two-track curriculum (i.e. a chance for people to be non-classicists). There were after all boys with scientific flair about, notably the incredible Alan Campbell Swinton, who in 1879 at the age of 15, after reading a description of the working of the telephone, invented only two years earlier, constructed a pair of telephones (apparently the first in Scotland) and linked up Glencorse and Moredun. They worked very well, but it was thought his absorption with science interfered with his Latin verse composition, and he had to send the telephones home. Nothing daunted, Swinton, the most inventive scientist of his day, presented the School in 1886 with a complete set of telephones. He went on to produce the first X-ray photographs in Britain and originate in 1908 an all-electronic concept for the realisation of television, having every claim to be seen as the father of modern, electronic television, as against Baird's short-lived mechanical system. In 1920, as an FRS, he expounded wireless telephony to the Royal Society.

By 1880 the School had a sanatorium, fives courts, a new terrace of six houses to the west between the School and the Poorhouse (Moredun Crescent), a debating society, a School magazine (*The Fettesian*, first published in April 1878) and a School song ('Floreas Fettesia'). D. W. Tanqueray had arrived to teach the First Form and begin his 47-year period on the staff. By 1884 he was running the newly opened 'waiting' House in Moredun Crescent, Kimmerghame.

The prefect system on the Rugby model was fully launched, and making life tough for the youngest boys. Prefects could be heavy-handed and boorish, but at the same time they could, when they wanted, stop their juniors being unkind to one another. A fairly tolerant atmosphere is reflected in the first letter home of Charles Henry Steel, just arrived as a 'new man' on May 13 1882, reporting that 'the boys did not tease us much.' His letter shows a philosophical approach both to discomfort and unappetising prep: 'My study is a dirty little hole, but I will soon have it all right. The cold bath was very nice. Most of the boys are very nice . . . I went to a class-room and got lessons for tonight, viz. *amo* and three chapters of Leviticus . . . Do not write too often, and I will not either.' This 'nice' picture may have been coloured for home consumption, but there is no talk of home-sickness or significant ill-treatment. The extent of actual bullying in the School is disputed. 'There was a good deal of bullying, both moral and physical,' wrote Gerald Campbell, but the youngest boys, once they came through 'the vale of tears' were 'as happy as kings.' Alfred Hamilton Grant's memories were rosier: 'The moral tone of Fettes was excellent and the general conduct amazingly good. The system of prefects worked admirably.' It did not eliminate completely the 'unnatural practices'

24

and rough behaviour found at so many of the older boarding schools, but the influence of the Headmaster prevented them from dominating. 'Those Fettes masters of my day,' recalled Henry Hamilton Fyfe, 'did make us feel that *noblesse oblige . . .* that there was a choice between behaving decently and behaving like cads.'

Potts' kindly influence was complemented by his wife, and their home was an island of domestic warmth in a community otherwise dominated by senior boys and bachelor masters. An invitation to the Lodge for breakfast was in prospect always terrifying for a small boy, but Ellen Potts could make him feel she was deeply interested in what he was doing. She knew how to bridge the gap between her Olympian spouse and the ordinary boy. Then there was their daughter, Carrie. Her image was something special in a community starved of attractive females. Very pretty, with sparkling eyes, a soft olive complexion and an enchanting smile, she seemed the perfection of girlhood. Stunned disbelief then greeted the news of her engagement to F. J. R. Hendy, a master who arrived in 1882 and was rapidly identified as a 'rasping' disciplinarian. She stood convicted of lack of taste, but the marriage worked out very happily.

There was a shadow over the Lodge, however. In early June 1883, a boy called Duncan Campbell died suddenly of diphtheria. Others fell ill, and one of them was the youngest Potts, Joseph, aged six. The whole School was hurriedly sent home, so that the College buildings could be examined and cleared of infection. After three weeks the boys were summoned back for the last month of the summer term not to the School, but to Windermere, where space had been found at Old College, and to which 12 teachers, 184 boys and 25 servants now moved, along with 100 iron bedsteads. The thrill of this re-assembling in such lovely surroundings was only broken by tragic news. Ellen Potts had also caught diphtheria nursing her youngest son, and both had died. The sorrow of the School was all too clear at the memorial service, and a decision was soon made to put up a memorial window to the Headmaster's wife in Chapel – the St Cecilia Window – which still recalls her musicianship and her piano-playing. She loved above all the music of Grieg, just then being published, and would accompany the Headmaster as he sang in his deep bass voice. This 'gracious and devoted lady' had played her part to the full in the birth of the School.

Meanwhile at Windermere, cricket was replaced by the climbing of Helvellyn and Scafell Pike. The food was better than in Edinburgh, and each morning there was the midday bathe to look forward to. It was almost idyllic. There was a new master to meet too, K. P. Wilson, destined to stay at Fettes for 40 years. Straightforward and full of life, he was, the boys decided at once, an asset.

It had to end. The School buildings were decontaminated by September, and when the boys re-assembled for the new school year, they found that old Dr Malcolm (who consistently prescribed revolting Gregory's Mixture for everything) had been replaced by Montagu Cotterill, whose pharmaceutics were more up to date. The interrupted routine was resumed.

Meanwhile, though, thunder clouds had been gathering over the Trustees. Within the city of Edinburgh, the original reception given to the School had been

Ellen Potts in the 1870s.

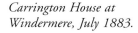

Carrington House at Windermere, July 1883.

*Moredun Crescent.
Kimmerghame House occupied
nos 5 and 6.*

in some quarters icy, but, in particular, noises of discontent had been rumbling among concerned locals for several years about the way Sir William Fettes' legacy had been administered. The will had left his estate 'for the maintenance, education and outfit of young people whose parents have either died without leaving sufficient funds for that purpose, or who from innocent misfortune during their lives are unable to give suitable education to their children.' The opening salvo came from *The Scotsman* newspaper in the mid-1870s. In a vitriolic article, the writer declared that the Foundationers at Fettes were not at all the penury-stricken Edinburgh children the founder had envisaged. They were 'the sons of decayed princes' living in 'Sardanapalian luxury.' The weird hyperbole baffled the boys. Used to spartan conditions of freezing cold and endless wind punctuated by bone-rattling team-games and uninspiring meals, they did not recognise their condition as one of Sardanapalian luxury (Sardanapalus being a transvestite Assyrian king of unimaginable wealth). In October 1883, however, the campaign gathered momentum. Duncan McLaren, former MP for Edinburgh, mounted an all-out attack on the Trustees in the columns of *The Daily Review*. In his view, a small group of self-elected trustees had subverted the Fettes Trust for the benefit of the male offspring of the professional classes. His main points were:

(1) The Fettes boys were too well-off. Sir William had clearly meant to help really poor children.
(2) The money had been grossly mismanaged. Far too much had been

spent on prestigious buildings (£227,644), leaving too little to pay for the schooling of really poor children. Bad planning had reduced the income to an inadequate £6,000 (from an original bequest of £166,000), as against, for example, the £25,000 generated annually by George Heriot's original bequest of £23,625.

(3) The non-Foundationers (the fee-paying boarders) were, by living in houses built by the Trust, being subsidised by a Trust meant only to help the poor.

(4) Even the 'necessitous' pupils, the Foundationers, were sons of gentlemen and came from the professional classes. Even they had to pay for their 'outfit', so were not fully subsidised anyway.

(5) There were no girls in the School. Sir William, by specifying 'young people', clearly intended it to be co-educational.

(6) Among the Trustees there were no women (though there were two on Sir William's original list) or representatives of trade, in which Sir William himself had been engaged.

Simmering in the background was the fact that the School was on an English model and contained English boys. The Trustees had, concluded McLaren, 'substituted an imitation English public school for the foundation devised by Fettes.'

The furore grew. A discussion at the 2nd November meeting of the Edinburgh Chamber of Commerce was led by John Gulland:

> As to the nature of the education the boys in Fettes College obtained, he must say that it seemed very desirable that any education given in Edinburgh should be of a distinctly Scotch character, and that it appeared to many of them that education given on the lines of Eton or Harrow was entirely out of place, and quite unnecessary in Scotland, where the education had been so distinctive, and regarding which no-one could say that it did not eventuate in very valuable results to Scotch boys.

The battle was long and fierce. Then, as at intervals since, there was within Edinburgh, mixed with admiration of the successes of the new School, a resentment

---

Dietary Scale.

Breakfast.—2 days salt meat, with tea or coffee, bread and butter.
       „   1 day eggs   „
       „   4 days slice of cold meat   „
Dinners.*—Sunday, Cold roast beef and potatoes.
      „   „   Cold fruit tart or hot plum-pudding.
      „   4 days   Hot roast meat and vegetables.
                 Puddings.
      „   1 day   Soup or fish.
                 Stewed meat, or meat pies and vegetables.
      „   „   Soup.
                 Cold meat (salt).
Tea.—Plain.
Supper.—Porridge, or bread and cheese with beer.

The healthy, basic meals of the 1870s.

of its Englishness, its air of superiority. Its building, too, was so assertive. Vast, ornate and unashamed, it drew the eye magnetically whenever you looked north-west from the city. 'Here I am,' it seemed to say. 'What are you going to do about it?'

The burghers of Edinburgh tried to do something about it. For a time the entire future of the School hung in the balance. The matter was taken up by the Educational Endowments (Scotland) Commission, which received a series of submissions, some attacking the Trustees, some warmly supportive, like the letter from Professor Ramsay of Glasgow (an Old Rugbeian). The achievements of the School, he argued, must be largely the product of the kind of school it was. Scotland needed more such, not fewer. 'Any crippling of Fettes College,' he concluded, 'would be a national misfortune.' There was pressure for Fettes to become a day-school, and this prospect so much worried the authorities at The Edinburgh Academy that they sent a Director, Andrew Beatson Bell, to support the Fettes Trustees in their efforts to remain a boarding establishment. One Commissioner even suggested that the Academy should be amalgamated with Fettes. 'I should not oppose that at all,' said Beatson Bell. Potts told the Commissioners that he had a few day-boys but it was not a success because parents never got up early enough to get their sons to school in time for the first class at 7.30 a.m.

Finally, in January 1885, the Commission published 'The Fettes Scheme'. The Commissioners had disagreed intensely. Even the sale of the building had been proposed, but finally the Scheme proposed a new Governing Body to replace the Trustees and a series of measures to focus the financial resources of the Trust more sharply on the 50 needy Foundationers. The Governing Body should even have 'full powers as early as may be to sell the whole of their landed estates . . . reserving only

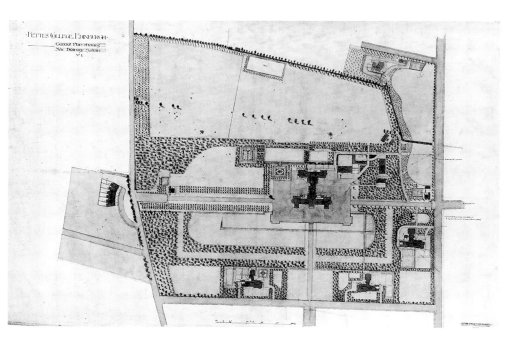

A map of the College grounds, 1883.

28

The view of the College from the east: an early print taken from a glass plate, c.1889.

such extent as may be required for the exercise and recreation of the scholars in attendance.' The objections of Edinburgh citizens were put to the Commission by Campbell ('Cocky') Lorimer, grandfather (ironically enough) of a later Headmaster of Fettes, Donald Crichton-Miller. He suggested that those benefiting from Sir William's will ought all to be from Scotland. 'Don't you think,' asked the Chairman impatiently, 'that if he had meant Scotch he would have said so?'

The fight was not yet over. Many thought the Scheme did not go nearly far enough. The Scotch Education Department approved it on 10th December 1885, and on the petition of the Free Church Presbytery it was laid before Parliament in February 1886. Meanwhile *The Scotsman* raised the temperature in another inflammatory article. The final onslaught came in a debate in the House at the end of March. Mr. J. Wilson, one of the members for Edinburgh, (strongly supported by the Irish Nationalists!) proposed in the early hours of Tuesday 30th March 'that an humble address be presented to Her Majesty asking her to withhold her assent.' After a stormy debate, the motion was rejected by 82 votes to 61, and the Fettes Scheme was approved by Order of Her Majesty in Council on 3rd April.

The Trustees were licking their wounds, but they were still in office. To replace the Board of Trustees as such, there was to be a new Governing Body, more broadly based. To the existing body of five were added the Lord Provost of Edinburgh, the Principal of the University, the Master of the Merchant Company, the Dean of the Faculty of Advocates, the Deputy Keeper of the Signet and the Minister of the High Kirk of St Giles. Future appointments to the Governing Body would also be

The dining hall set for Christmas dinner, 1889.

made, as vacancies arose, by the Senators of the College of Justice, the Chamber of Commerce and the Royal College of Physicians of Edinburgh.

The implications for the Trustees themselves were inescapable. The day-to-day running of the School, however, was little affected by the changes to its constitution, and its reputation and its numbers continued to grow. By 1887 there were 173 boys – 108 from Scotland, 63 from England, one from Ireland and one from Italy. It was above all the general confidence in Potts' management that had brought the School through its crisis virtually intact. His personal qualities had played their part too. No-one, after all, could claim that Potts was the sort of man to be thoughtless of the needs of the poor in society. In a sermon to the 1885 leavers, he had said:

> There is, I am sure, a rustling among the leaves which is the prelude to a great wind of change . . . There is a feeling arising within the Universities themselves and the Public Schools that these seats of learning with their stores of wealth and literature have somehow not done enough for the morality and life of the country at large. There are certain great social evils . . . The youth of our Public Schools . . . are bound, as they have freely received, freely to give, and not to allow the poor . . . to be fed, or housed, or worked in a way prejudicial to health, happiness and the dignity of human nature.

The work of the School was to be inspected in the future by Government-appointed examiners. The first examination in August 1887 produced a glowing report of 'an admirable school' under 'a Headmaster of exceptional ability', concluding with Dr Jex-Blake's words: 'In the interest of Scotland and of Education alike, Fettes College should be let alone; and Dr. Potts should be supported in the uncontrolled control of a noble College, which owes him much and will owe him more.' The echoes of the battle, though, (known to some as The Citizens' Revolt) were still resonating decades later. In 1925 Freddy Macdonald, newly arrived to join the staff, took a charabanc tour to acquaint himself with the city he had come to. As the coach passed Fettes, he was surprised to hear the driver say: 'Yon's Fettes College, founded to educate the sons of the poor. How the hell it got into the hands of the rich, I dinna ken.'

In 1887 there were two shocks. At the end of Evensong one Sunday in May, the thunderous chords from the organ of the chorus from *Judas Maccabaeus* stopped abruptly. 'Huxty', the School organist, had died at the keyboard. Then in a freak accident during a game of 'broomstick cricket' on the evening of Founder's Day, K. P. Wilson severed his femoral artery. He was saved by the presence of a young doctor who held the ends together for half an hour, and by D. W. Tanqueray who later gave blood for the crucial transfusion. The dying man recovered, to serve Fettes for another 38 years. In the same year, Cecil Reddie, who had been boy and master at the School, left to set up a new school at Abbotsholme. The eccentric Reddie was a seminal figure in the growth of progressive education, and Abbotsholme was run on pioneering, pupil-centred lines. His influence spread when one of his masters left to start Bedales, and when Kurt Hahn happened to meet two Abbotsholme boys on a climbing holiday in Switzerland. His long conversation with them strengthened his resolve to open his remarkable school at Salem, destined to give birth in time to others like Gordonstoun.

As the 1880s wore on, school life was becoming more diversified. On the games field, hockey and fives (the Rugby version, of course) were building up. The athletic Games were held in spring with an enthusiasm sharpened by the knowledge that two Fettesians had already become English Amateur Champions in their events (Edgar Storey in the quarter mile in 1879, John Parsons in the high jump in 1880 and 1883, and in the long jump in 1883). Tennis was played but was frowned on, as 'you did no-one good but yourself' in playing it. Few forms of exercise, however, were remembered in the after-school years so vividly as the Paperchase, when the Hares set off into the open country that still lay all round the School, scattering bits of paper behind them as scent, heading for the Firth of Forth or the Pentland Hills. The runs could be as long as 25 miles. 'I recall' wrote Hamilton Fyfe, 'the golden warmth of the September afternoons . . . the beauty of autumn woods, the glistening furrows of newly-ploughed fields across which we ran, the River Almond rippling serene and shallow over its pebbly bed, the jog-trot homewards in the crisp brightness of early evening, the welcome sousing and rub-down in dimly lighted dressing-room, and then the House Tea – with toasted scones or cookies and unlimited jam.'

The Headmaster, too, stayed as active as ever and loved to walk whenever he could. In November 1889, however, came a walk too far. For the Loretto match that autumn, Potts walked all the way down to Musselburgh to watch. After the

Athletics in 1893. Top: *the high jump,* middle: *hurdles,* below: *the sack race.*

match he began the seven-mile walk back, but suddenly found himself in excruciating pain. By the time he got home, he was in a serious condition. Montagu Cotterill the School doctor was called and diagnosed 'strangulation of the intestines.' Eminent surgeons were consulted, but the medical skill of the day did not extend to an abdominal operation, nor indeed anything much more than quicksilver by the mouth, a drastic remedy supposed to break down the blockage. It did no good, and the unthinkable news now started to circulate among the boys that their Headmaster was dying. 'The shadow of death was over the School,' recalled Hamilton Grant, 'and boys whispered together in awed little groups.'

Potts had hoped to finish his time at Fettes, seek ordination and then find a small country living in England where he could teach children in Parish Schools the Bible story. It was a humble ambition, but it was not to be. His achievement, though, had been astonishing. In 19 years he had established his School as the premier Scottish public school, and set it academically and on the games field in the forefront of the schools of the kingdom. He had won the deep respect of boys, masters and parents. There can be no doubt that Potts was among the greatest headmasters of the 19th century.

'Cut off in the fullness of his powers, with the fabric of a great work growing under his hand' (Hamilton Grant), he was resigned and full of faith. The last entry in his Commonplace Book was a quotation from Fichte:

> 'Whatever man may do, so long as he does it from himself as a finite being, by himself and through his own counsel – it is vain and will sink to nothing. Only when a foreign power takes possession of him and urges him forward and lives in him in room [place] of his own energy, does true and real existence take up its abode in his life. This foreign power is ever the power of God.'

The Chapel in the 1880s.

On his death-bed Potts still found time to send the Head of School a note saying how sorry he was not to be able to give him some final help to prepare him for the Balliol Scholarship he was due to sit in a few days. He was far from depressing company for those who sat by his bed. He was ready to go, he said, as he had paid all his bills. He even reminded them of ironical death-bed remarks like that of the Emperor Vespasian, *Vae! divus fio.* ('Dear me! I'm turning into a god.') The end came as the boys were going into lunch on 15th November 1889. After the meal, games were cancelled and they were all called into Chapel, where the masters joined them. After a short wait, the Head of School, Alfred Hamilton Grant, came in and walked up to the lectern. He told them their Headmaster had just died and had left a message for them all. 'Such was the manner,' wrote Lord Simon who was in Chapel that day, 'in which this prince of teachers, though racked with pain, sought to discharge his task amongst us at the last.' The message, said Eric Anderson in his 1989 Potts Memorial Lecture, 'was not intended to be enshrined on marble. It was not intended for posterity, but for the boys in the School at the time, each one of whom Potts knew. The effect on them of that last message was profound.' They listened silently as Grant read out to them the words which Potts had dictated to Dr Cotterill:

I wish particularly to offer to all the boys at Fettes College my grateful acknowledgments of their loyalty, affection and generous appreciation of me.

Then, in words which now stand in the School Chapel and have been read by Fettesians of every generation, he went on:

I wish as a dying man to record that mercy and loving-kindness have followed me all the days of my life; that firm faith in God is the sole stay in mortal life; that all other ideas but Christ are illusory; and that duty is the one and sole thing worth living for.

'The world,' wrote his obituarist at Shrewsbury, 'could have better spared many a more famous man.'

A silhouette of Potts from the 1880s.

Potts' last message, as dictated, an hour before his death, to Dr Montagu Cotterill.

"Sub tegmine fagi".

J. W. Parsons.

The Cricket Field with the Yeo Pavilion in the background: wash drawing by J. W. Parsons.

3

Thirty Years of Consolidation
HEARD : 1890–1919

The death of Potts left a vacuum at the heart of the School. A 'Patriarch' writing later to *The Fettesian* remembered that for weeks after he heard his old Headmaster had died he was haunted by the lines of Browning:

> We that had loved him so, followed him, honoured him,
>   Lived in his mild and magnificent eye,
> Learned his great language, caught his clear accents,
>   Made him our pattern to live and to die.

The person who missed him most was his friend, long-time colleague and deputy Clem Cotterill. On the evening of Potts' funeral (19th November 1889), James Edwards wrote home from Carrington: 'Poor old Clem seemed more cut up about it than anybody. After the body was lowered he stood weeping over the grave for at least a quarter of an hour.' But Cotterill did not just weep for Potts, he wanted to succeed him. Together they had planned the new School, and they shared the same liberal views. Cotterill had given 20 years of his life to Fettes, and saw his own succession as ensuring a seamless continuation of the ideals of its first Headmaster. Not everyone agreed. Cotterill was much loved, a visionary and a natural democrat who identified with the boys. The Governors, however, were not sure about his discipline and suspected the unconventional tinge of his opinions. They were looking for someone with dignity and detachment. Further, they knew of such a man, through his service as Housemaster of School House (1872–75) and Carrington (1875–85), and when they sent to the Dean of Westminster for advice, he sent back to them one and the same name.

The Reverend William Augustus Heard was educated at Manchester Grammar School and Trinity College, Oxford. He had first come to Fettes in 1871, and had then gone on to Westminster in 1885 as Second Master. Known earlier in Carrington for a mixture of detachment, fairness, sarcasm and strong discipline, he ran his House like clockwork He lacked Cotterill's warmth, but had the strong administrative grip the Governors wanted. He was also a fine scholar and teacher. He was appointed Headmaster at the end of 1889. He knew all too well that Potts was a hard act to follow. In his first sermon in Chapel as Headmaster he said:

William Augustus Heard as a young man.

The swimming baths before and after the fire of 1890.

The central figure is gone. He is gone whose rich personality gave colour to the whole scene . . . .and it must be hard for you to recognise the place that knows him no more.

The main colour Heard contributed to the scene was black, if Robert Bruce Lockhart's first impressions are anything to go by:

> His hair was black; his eyebrows and sidewhiskers were black, his high-cut coat was black; his trousers were black; his gown was black. The only relief to the general blackness was provided by the white collar and the heavy gold chain across his waistcoat.

One of his nicknames, indeed, was The Black Beetle. Sadly, his wife had died two years earlier at Westminster, and he arrived at the School as a widower with a family of two boys and three girls. He threw himself into the new job and, though at first it was hard to compensate for the fact that he was not Potts, he rapidly established a firm grip. William McClure noticed 'his quiet smile, his extraordinary air of authority.' His warmer side came through to the classical Sixth Form and the School prefects, and at breakfasts in the Lodge he was a genial host, though these occasions were certainly improved by the presence of his three daughters. To the rank and file of the School he was always a remote figure, glimpsed in the dining hall or on the opposite touch-line at a rugby match, rarely met – an 'Olympian dynast', inhabiting a different planet. Hence the incredulity of the School when it was reported that 'The Bulge' (one of Heard's nicknames) had been seen riding a bicycle. The association of him and such a mundane pursuit was beyond their imagination.

The School he took over in January 1890 was in excellent shape, and the numbers reached 211 later in the year. Life was still spartan in the extreme, without electricity or proper central heating, but Heard struck a tiny blow for comfort in 1890 by supplying cocoa before early school. At first Heard was much occupied with the question of a memorial to Dr Potts. Two thousand pounds was quickly raised, and there was much talk of actually erecting a new chapel in his memory. By 1891, though, the decision was made to use the fund for an exhibition and a Memorial window in the Chapel.

36

Disappointed at not succeeding to the Headship, Cotterill soon left Fettes. In 1890 he was invited to take over the helm at Greenpark School, Liverpool, a school which he ran until he retired in 1898. This meant finding a new housemaster for Glencorse, and G. C. Harrison arrived with glowing testimonials from Clifton. Carrington, under John Yeo, was meanwhile enlarged to take 50 boys. On 16th May of Heard's first year, the School swimming bath was gutted by fire, but quickly rebuilt. In 1896, another fire, started by a Bunsen burner in the science laboratory, led to the construction of new laboratories in the North Building, and a carpenter's workshop in the old stable yard. To a man more scientifically inclined than Heard this would have given a chance to expand the science provision, but, though teaching conditions were much improved, it did little to raise the status of the subject.

In 1894 and again in 1899, the Governors bought land north of the Jordan burn which in time was to provide much more games-playing space. Although Heard lacked the attributes of a natural games player, he was not the man to challenge the cult of athleticism. The cult was always going to grow if left up to the boys, and it had reached such extravagant proportions at some public schools that headmasters were looking for ways to damp it down. But Heard knew that the phenomenal reputation of the School on the games field, and at rugby in particular, was a key ingredient in its public image, and he was determined to sustain it. New games were allowed to gain a foothold, and K. P. Wilson started hockey. In 1891 a game between Fettes and Loretto was organised which was the first recorded hockey match in Scotland. Cricket was helped by useful players like Hesketh Prichard, who was asked to play for Scotland while still at school, but had to refuse since the game clashed with the Loretto match, while Malcolm Jardine, who had just left, was proving himself the best cricketer the School was to produce. The performance of the rugby XV had shown signs of a dip in 1890, and in 1893 Heard appointed the first games master at Fettes, Charles Fleming, who had left Carrington six years earlier. The one pure Scot on the staff, he was to gain two Scottish caps at rugby, and before the 1897 Calcutta Cup match could be found swinging on the Fettes

Below left: the College building after the fire of 1896 (the labs were on the top floor of the east wing); below: a chemistry laboratory in the North Building after the fire.

37

parallel bars to get his weight down to 15 st. 9 lb. Between 1893 and 1900 he reorganised the games structure, and laid the foundations for the dramatic resurgence in Fettes' rugby reputation after that. He started 'House Belows' in 1894 and 'Cricket Leagues' in 1896, both for the less gifted player. House Belows were destined to become a Fettes institution, notorious for the ferocity with which they were played, supposedly leading in later years to a request from the Western General Hospital for a Fettes calendar, so that they could keep a bed free on House Below days. Mothers of prospective Fettesians who happened to visit while they were going on were known to withdraw their sons' names on the spot.

As a rugby-playing nation, Scotland was ahead of the other home countries during this period (three wins ahead of England, four of Wales and 15 of Ireland), and within the School the atmosphere was heavily impregnated with the rugby culture. At house prayers the prefects chose special hymns before and after key matches, more as tribal songs than in the irreverent supposition that the deity favoured the home team. Before the Merchiston or Loretto match there was 'Christian, seek not yet repose' or 'Fight the good fight'. If Fettes won, they sang 'For all the saints who from their labours rest'. Members of the 1st XV could have privileges like beer after matches, but some declined as their fitness might be impaired. The cult was reinforced by the Edinburgh newspapers, which stoked up to excess the fervour centring on the school rugby Championship. It was fought out by the six public schools of Scotland, each playing each other twice. On Fridays the *Evening News* or the *Evening Dispatch* used to survey the prospects for the next day's games, with reports on them in Saturday's late editions and on Monday. They went in for headlines like 'Schoolboys Astounding', and the ball was referred to as the 'oblong' or the 'spheroid'. The matches at Loretto received heavy support from Musselburgh fishermen and miners, who at key moments might hurl abuse at the Fettes players, and even chunks of turf or fish. 'The immense force of rivalry', according to a 1911 article by George Wade in the *Boys' Own Paper* ('The Greatest of Football Schools'), 'has gone far towards making Fettes what she is today in football'. Recalling the most thrilling moments he has witnessed in school sport, Wade says that 'even these were mild scenes compared with the day when I stood watching Fettes and Loretto struggle with two magnificent fifteens for the mastery.' Though the slump in Fettes'

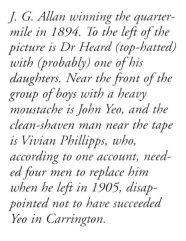

J. G. Allan winning the quarter-mile in 1894. To the left of the picture is Dr Heard (top-hatted) with (probably) one of his daughters. Near the front of the group of boys with a heavy moustache is John Yeo, and the clean-shaven man near the tape is Vivian Phillipps, who, according to one account, needed four men to replace him when he left in 1905, disappointed not to have succeeded Yeo in Carrington.

Masters at the Below Fields fence, sometime between 1895 and 1904. A. F. Bohuslav-Kroupa is sitting on the fence, David Tanqueray is standing next to him and Vivian Phillipps is holding his knee. John Yeo is sitting cross-legged on Phillipps' right. On the far right of the picture is Harry Pyatt.

1st XV performance lasted for much of the 1890s, by 1902 the tide had decisively turned.

This process was helped by the appointment of two Cambridge rugby Blues, R. F. Cumberlege in 1902 and G. H. Keeton in 1903. Under their guidance the XV went from strength to strength, and between the spring of 1902 and February 1906 it remained undefeated and the Fettes line was crossed only twice. A lull in 1906 and 1907 was followed by a further run of victories in 1908 and 1909. Wade's description of Fettes as the Greatest of Football Schools was prompted by the fact that (as before in 1890) both the Oxford and Cambridge XVs of 1909 were captained by Fettesians (who both also gained First Class degrees). He puts down Fettes' pre-eminence to (1) excellence in pitches, practice arrangements and coaching (by old boys as well as others), (2) the enthusiasm and encouragement that makes every boy want to do well and get into the 1st XV if he can, and (3) tremendous local opposition. Fettes teams, he believed, are also good at exploiting conditions: '"Bigside", the chief ground at Fettes, has a "trick-piece" towards the northern end, which Fettesians understand too well, and on which they have won many a victory by rushing the opposing forces ere the latter has grasped the position of affairs.'

In March 1906 the Scottish team contained six Old Fettesians, while a seventh was selected but had to withdraw through injury. Most remarkable of all the sportsmen of this time was K. G. Macleod. Known as 'Grunt', he was an athlete of phenomenal gifts, whose running was described by the *Evening News* as 'the poetry of motion.' He first played for the School at 14, and a couple of years later was summoned by Heard, who said 'Macleod, if you were asked to play for Scotland, what would you say?' 'I would say that I was too young, Sir.' 'Good! because that is just what I told the selectors this morning.' The Scottish XV in fact came for a practice

The view of Edinburgh from the College tower, drawn by E. Burrow, 1901.

John Yeo, who died in harness in 1904.

match against Fettes (with two masters added) in January 1905, and after a hard game won 20 - 6. Macleod's sporting career was short but remarkable. The try he scored for the Scotland XV to beat South Africa in the 1906 match at Hampden was, some thought, 'the most dramatic of all time.'

The second decade of Heard's reign brought the deaths of three outstanding schoolmasters, G. C. Harrison (double First, cricket Blue, Housemaster of Glencorse) in March 1900, R. W. Broadrick, killed in a fall from Pinnacle Rock, Scafell in September 1903, and finally in 1904 John Yeo, Housemaster of Carrington. As a schoolmaster, Yeo was pure gold. He was a father to the boys of Carrington and they were devoted to him. He hated to punish. 'The severest punishment we received,' recalled James Herriot, 'was the knowledge that we had hurt him.' He was no athlete, but he loved to push himself physically along with his boys. He was always at the House nets or on the 'puntabout' after prep, and he liked fielding on a raw day at cover point or going for the School run in a blizzard. When he died of pneumonia at the age of 44 he had spent half his life at Fettes. 'It may safely be said,' ran his obituary in *The Scotsman*, 'that amongst the House Masters of public schools, few have died so universally beloved.' The School was stunned, and Heard began his memorial sermon with the words: 'There are times when life seems all amiss, all bewilderment, all perplexity.' Yeo's memorial still stands: the cricket Pavilion, completed in 1906.

The immediate problem for Heard, however, was his replacement in Carrington. The outstanding candidate to succeed him as Housemaster appeared to be Vivian Phillipps, modern linguist and musician, who had been at Fettes for 11 years. A fine teacher and talented contributor to School music and staff drama, he kept effortless discipline, without having to beat or give impositions. The sarcastic tinge to his wit

40

A rugby house match (Schoolhouse v. Carrington), 26th November
1879: watercolour by J. W. Parsons.

Above: *the Pipe Band beating Retreat on Founder's Day 1992.*

Right: *members of CCF by the War Memorial.*

certainly helped. Some masters found it hard to stop their classes peering out of the window when at intervals the School entertained the inmates of the Poorhouse (located on the site of the modern Western General Hospital) and they straggled up the west drive during class time. Phillipps simply announced, 'Any boy who wishes to look at his parents may get up and look out of the window.' Phillipps' abilities made him in many people's eyes the obvious man to take over in Carrington, 'the best house in the School' at that time, but to his dismay Heard appointed Harry Pyatt. It was a fateful decision for Carrington since Pyatt was to stay there for 30 years. Phillipps (a bachelor modern linguist) was convinced that Pyatt was appointed over him because he was a married classicist, and, indeed, Pyatt had strengthened his claim by winning the hand of Fanny, the daughter of the Bishop of Edinburgh. The episode led to wide questioning of Heard's judgement and to the loss of Vivian Phillipps to Fettes. He left to become a barrister, MP for Edinburgh West, Liberal Chief Whip and Chairman of the Liberal Party's Central Organisation. He promised to return to Fettes at the head of a procession carrying a banner with the words 'To Hell with the Properispomenon' (a somewhat trying Greek accent and a symbol, in Phillipps' eyes, of the dominance of the Classics).

For the Classics still reigned unchallenged. The Headmaster was himself a classicist and a gifted teacher, and little happened during his long reign to disturb the subject's pre-eminent position in the curriculum. Since Potts had given way to 'bifurcation' in 1878, it had long been possible for those with a passion for history, geography or science to avoid Latin and Greek in the Sixth Form, but every step was taken to prevent those who did so ('the Mods') from enjoying any sort of standing in the community. Heard called them 'barbarians', and *The Fettesian* carried a series of plaintive letters from them complaining that they were not allowed to sit at the Sixth Form table at lunch or have hot milk. John Hay Beith, a Fettesian himself and a master 1900–01 and 1906–12, wrote soon after leaving a series of

The cricket Pavilion, the College's memorial to John Yeo.

41

David Tanqueray, who was at Fettes for 47 years, from 1879 to 1926.

A caricature of Tanqueray.

articles in Blackwood's Magazine which were then brought together and published in 1914 as *The Lighter Side of School Life* under the name Ian Hay. It is a distillation in caricature of his reactions to Fettes life. Of the scientific Mods he writes:

> Time was when A Sound Classical Education, Lady Matron and Meat for Breakfast formed the alpha and omega of a public school prospectus. But times have changed, at least in so far as the Sound Classical Education is concerned . . . First of all, the members of that once despised race, the teachers of Science. Formerly these maintained a servile and apologetic existence . . . Now they have uprisen, and, asseverating that classical education is a pricked bubble, ask boldly for expensive apparatus and a larger tract of space in the timetable.

The views of the Parent and the Boy were also starting to be taken into account. This was a dangerous innovation, but Heard was fairly impervious to such stirrings, and as it happened the Mods, in addition to being denied privileges, were seldom taught in an inspiring way. The modern side covered English, history, geography, languages, chemistry and physics. Biology was not taught, except that T. B. Franklin, who taught maths, would take a week off now and then either to do meteorology, or to dissect sheep's eyes which he obtained from the butcher. Geography, history and English were covered by David Tanqueray, Housemaster of Moredun, who spent 47 years at Fettes. Once you had reached the Upper Fifth Mods, you might spend one, two or even three years in his class. Tanqueray had a poetry exam every Saturday, but as the papers were the same every year and each house kept its own set of copies, its terrors were few. Tanqueray's method apparently imprinted his sayings in the minds of his pupils, though his advice was not always relevant to their situation. He told third-formers, for example, never to accept gifts sent by tradespeople to secure custom. 'When I was sent a free case of champagne,' he would say, 'I returned it.'

One thing that drove boys on to the modern side was the prospect of entering the Upper Fifth (classical). They would test themselves against its demands and find themselves wanting. The class was so formidable, such a maelstrom of activity that the less ambitious opted for a quiet life in the placid, if tedious pastures of the modern side. The classical Upper Fifth was presided over by K. P. Wilson, the greatest of all Fettes characters. In *The Lighter Side of School Life* he is thinly disguised as 'Mr. Dumaresq'. He approaches the formroom:

> 'Greek prose scraps!' he roared, while still ten yards from the door. Instantly each boy seized a sheet of school paper, and having torn it into four pieces selected one of the pieces and waited, pen in hand.
> '*If you do this,*' announced Mr. Dumaresq truculently as he swung into the doorway, '*you will be wise.*'
> Every boy began to scribble madly.
> '*If you do not do this,*' continued Mr. Dumaresq, '*you will not be wise. If you were to do this you would be wise. If you were not to do this you would not be wise. If you had done this you would have been wise. If you had not done this you would not have been wise.* Collect!'
> The head boy sprang to his feet, and feverishly dragging the scraps from under the

hands of his panting colleagues, laid them on the master's desk. Like lightning Mr. Dumaresq looked them over. 'Seven of you ignorant of the construction of the simplest conditional sentence!' he bellowed. 'Come in this afternoon.'

K. P. (known invariably by his initials) had a First in Classics at Cambridge and had been a brilliant athlete there, but he despised the 'blood' who thought that nothing but games mattered. Glencorse boys worshipped him. They loved his post-Chapel symposia, when cocoa and cakes were consumed and books and politics dissected. 'What he liked in boys,' wrote John Stevenson, 'was originality and initiative.' He made no effort to ingratiate himself with the parents of his boys. On one boy's report he wrote: 'Dull, plodding, platitudinous – would make a good parent.' 'I've brought up five boys,' declared one mother. K. P. replied, 'Madam, I've brought up hundreds.' Every afternoon he could be seen tramping the grounds, scruffily dressed and wearing shorts ('cuts') accompanied by his bull terrier Bobby, with a bag on his back to collect sheep's droppings for his garden. Although back in 1887 his life had been saved by a transfusion of blood supplied by David Tanqueray, the two men, who were at Fettes together for over 40 years and ran neighbouring houses, were ironically at daggers drawn. Tanqueray ran Moredun on extremely traditional lines but was highly respected by his boys. Immaculate in spats, he was known as the Lord, or Tink. He kept exactly to the standard procedure for everything, in contrast with K. P., who was all for the spirit rather than the letter of the law.

A caricature of K. P. Wilson.

School House had been run briefly in the 1890s by A. S. Ramsey, a fine mathematician who went on in 1897 to become Fellow and, later, President of Magdalene College, Cambridge, married K. P. Wilson's sister and became father of a future Archbishop of Canterbury. The regime there kept changing until J. S. Edwards (known as 'Pow' because of the Cockney way he pronounced words like pound) gave it some continuity by staying for 15 years (joined, late in the War, by Jim Rhoades, whose study, said Walter Sellar, 'was an oasis of real civilisation'). Edwards had had a disconcerting start in 1902. At his interview, held at Carlisle railway station, Heard appointed him on the spot and said 'It would be an advantage if you could teach some chemistry.' Since 'Pow' was a mathematician, this meant that he had to spend the whole summer working on this subject, only to be told on arrival at Fettes by Heard that he had meant to say physics! His sharp mind connected well with the brighter mathematicians, and he was to stay at Fettes for 42 years, taking over Glencorse from K. P. in 1925.

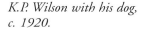

K.P. Wilson with his dog, c. 1920.

In the first decade of the 20th century the School's reputation remained high. Cargilfield prep school, then located in the Trinity area of Edinburgh, was offered to Fettes but in the end no deal was struck. 1907–9 in particular were golden years. Apart from all the successes in Classics, five Cambridge awards were won in this decade in mathematics, the only other strong subject at Fettes at this time. 'Dr Heard was at the height of his powers,' wrote Sir John Spencer Muirhead, later to distinguish himself in the Army and the Law. 'As a master he was in the first rank ... At the end of their time here Fettesians at Oxford or Cambridge found themselves more than half-way to classical degrees before they started to read for them. No English school surpassed, and no Scottish school came within measurable distance

The reception at the Lodge after the wedding of one of Dr Heard's daughters, c.1910. Dr Heard is in the centre of the picture, looking down at the ground. The man nearest the camera is W. T. Heard, the future Cardinal.

A. F. Bohuslav-Kroupa in his Art Room.

of, Fettes at this time as a classical school.' Heard's favourite reading was Aristophanes, whose comedies provided scope for the exercise of his heavily-veiled but mordant wit. The dominance of Oxbridge in the thinking of the School is illustrated by the figures for the 1909 leavers. 20 per cent went to Oxford or Cambridge and 13 per cent to Scottish Universities.

Classes were orderly, with perhaps two exceptions. The Art Class of A. F. Bohuslav-Kroupa was known to descend into pandemonium. This charming, extraordinary character came from Bohemia. 'The peculiar shape of his head,' recalled James Herriot, 'was reported to be the result of contact with a gun-carriage at the battle of Königgratz.' Others thought he had been scalped by a Prussian sabre. He was a most unlikely person to have ended up at Fettes. After joining the Austrian army he fought on the losing side in wars between Russia and Poland and between Germany and Austria, being left for dead on the field of Sadowa. He lived with the Indians in America, and joined the first band of pioneers who crossed Canada to explore the line for the great Canadian Pacific Railway. Set upon by brigands in Mexico, he lost everything, and had to take any kind of job he could find. Taking a boat for Cuba on impulse, he caught 'Yellow Jack' and almost died. He finally found his way to Scotland to teach Art. His incredible pre-Fettes career, however, failed to awe his classes into quiescence. 'Wild scuffles took place under desks, and projectiles skimmed through the air. Once a pea-shooter – aimed at someone else – exploded on his bald head. "I am shote, I am shote" cried he, and ran out into the arms of the Head.' His reports sometimes revealed his irritation, and were more candid than would be normal today. In one he wrote: 'He is a horrid little boy. I hate him.' The Reverend George Lenox-Conyngham, Housemaster of Kimmerghame for 19 years and the first old boy to come back to teach, was likewise not a disciplinarian. Happenings in his class (the Lower Fourth) included

44

lockers bursting into flames, fireworks going off, an explosion which wrecked the fireplace and the sabotaging of the gas lighting so that, after a given interval, the globe would burst into fragments above his head. A feature of his Greek teaching was 'the choral chanting of paradigms accompanied by a *tripudium* which shook College like an earthquake.' It worked. Robert Bruce Lockhart wrote: 'I shall remember those paradigms until I die.' Lenox-Conyngham (who later on was a passenger on the *Titanic* but sensibly disembarked at Cork) was in fact a rather saintly figure who preached memorable, dreamy sermons in a falsetto voice on texts like 'Wheresoever the carcase is, there will the eagles be gathered together.'

A key figure in school was the College porter, and Fettes porters were immensely loyal. William Skinner, the first porter, served for 52 years, but even this record was passed by the legendary George Perry ('Caesar') who arrived as houseboy in Carrington in 1905, took over as porter from Skinner and stayed until 1958. No less loyal were Sergeant Adam, who took gym for 38 years, and Geordie Howell, indefatigable groundsman and cricket professional from 1885 to 1919. The 'house men' looked after things in the houses, cleaning boys' shoes and keeping boxes of biscuits for distribution, since Heard had put out of bounds Haddow's Dairy in Crewe Road (a mecca for the boys with its scones and cream) and there was no tuck shop.

Each house was its own kingdom still, and life, grim and hard in your first year, improved as you went up the rungs of the house ladder to become, first of all, a 'dook', and then a prefect. 'Probably the new boy,' the *Public School* magazine of 1902 tells us, 'expects all kinds of terrors in the dormitory, but he finds only two.'

Sergeant Adam in the School Museum.

The Old Library c. 1890.

45

A boy (Kenneth Sanderson) in top hat and tailcoat, still being worn in 1937.

Below: *boys in Glencorse study area, 1909; below right: dormitory cubicles in the 1890s (note the tin bath in the bottom left-hand corner), although they were still like this in 1939.*

These were having to sing to the prefects and doing a 'circle', later known as a 'bar'. This meant pulling yourself up to a horizontal bar in the dormitory and swinging your legs over it. 'In some cases a hair-brush or strop are found to be marvellously useful in helping a laggard round the bar.' This became a ritual for the whole house after the rugby match against Loretto (sometimes abused by the wrong sort of prefects) and lasted until recent times. Knowing your place was the essential talent, and 'side' (presumption) the worst vice. There was little real comfort to be had, but school life wasn't about comfort. 'Fettes education in my time', wrote Bruce-Lockhart, 'was, above all things, virile.' Hygiene was still rudimentary. Each cubicle had in it a jug of cold water and a tin bath. You were allowed a 15-minute hot bath once a fortnight, unless you arranged to share the water with someone and have seven and a half minutes weekly. Lighting was very poor, and did no favours to your eyes as they strained to read, while the desks and chairs were so uncomfortable that they induced the phenomenon of the 'Fettes stoop'. In this Spartan *milieu*, however, there were still pleasures to be had. 'What shall be said,' asked Walter Sellar (author of *1066 and All That*) 'of those huge Form room fires, tiny flickerings at 7.30 a.m. but vast volcanoes of flame by 9 o'clock, or those brews of cocoa and Swiss milk in the evenings, or long afternoons of skating on Granton reservoir, or whole Sundays lounged away in peace and plenty in friends' houses in Edinburgh?' In Sunday afternoons in summer, the Green Walk was the place to be, as the *Public School Magazine* for 1902 tells us: 'Chairs, books, biscuits, fruit, and lemonade *ad lib* are brought out, and the joy of these things is great and sinks deep into the heart, until the cruel clanging of the bell breaks in.' Outings were fairly few, but the walk to Sunday church was a byword among the locals, as Fettesians processed in top hats and tailcoats with obligatory umbrellas to St Stephen's, Stockbridge, or (if you were a 'Pisky') Trinity Church on the Dean Bridge, then later on to St John's, Princes Street, where Canon Perry thundered against the Germans from his pulpit.

For the Germans were starting to loom in the consciousness of the boys. In

The first contingent of the Officers' Training Corps parading under John Hay Beith ('Ian Hay'), who became Major General Beith, 1909.

1908 an Officers' Training Corps had been started under Captain T. B. Franklin, perhaps in response to Field-Marshal Lord Roberts' appeal to the youth of the nation to be prepared to defend their country. It was decided that the kilt should be worn, and the Hunting Macleod tartan was chosen (the first Senior Cadet Officer being Norman Macleod Adams, who was to die in the War near Arras). The 1st Shooting VIII went to Bisley in 1908, and the Pipe Band was formed in 1912. The operations of the OTC became steadily more determined, but before the distant clouds of war had fully gathered there was a mysterious invasion from much closer to home in the early hours of 21st August 1913. A group of suffragettes broke into College by smashing a window in the Call-over Hall and started a fire on the first floor, at the door of the Headmaster's teaching room (now the Upper). It was blazing away when the School painters came in at 6 a.m. They seized the nearest fire hose, and by the time the horse-drawn fire brigade had arrived from another fire at Grange Loan, the fire was well under control. One third of the floor of the room was burnt out, together with the door of the next room. The damage (which included the loss of Dr. Potts' portrait) was estimated at £304, but as the painters were about to do the room anyway, the insurance claim was graciously reduced to £249.19.7. *The Fettesian* does not identify the arsonists. They were to be denied the 'oxygen of publicity', and the true nature of the incident was reported only in the *Suffragettes Weekly*. If the citizens of Edinburgh had been treated to the spectacle of this vast building going up in an inferno of flame on the northern skyline, it might have brought women's suffrage starkly into the public consciousness. As it was, Fettes posterity owes a debt to the School painters.

In 1913 came the news of the death of the first Fettesian VC. Matthew Meiklejohn had won 'the best VC of the Boer War' in October 1899, single-handedly rallying the

'The Fag: sic vos non vobis', drawing by Lewis Baumer, from Ian Hay's The Lighter Side of School Life, *published in 1914.*

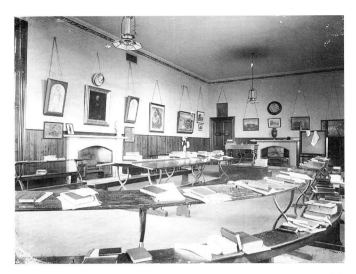

Above: *the Upper before 1890: note the horseshoe desk. The Headmaster taught the Classical Sixth here, from the desk in front of the far fireplace.*
Above right: *the Upper after it was set on fire by suffragettes on 21st August, 1913.*

The Anderson Memorial panel, Sandhurst.

wavering Gordon Highlanders at the battle of Elandslaagte. He had lost an arm in the action, and when on parade in Hyde Park on 28th June 1913, his horse bolted. With his one arm he just managed to turn it away from a line of troops, but then realised it was heading for a group of children. A few yards short of them he wrenched his frantic horse aside, but the only place to go was straight into the railings of Rotten Row. The horse was killed and Meiklejohn died six days later. His bravery was to be emulated by other Fettesians in the next few years.

War finally broke out during the summer camp of 1914 at Barry. The boys woke up one morning to find the CO and the Adjutant had abandoned them for their regiments. War was to have a number of effects on school life, but for the boys at first the clockwork routine of the School day kept it at arm's length. As time went on and it came home to the senior boys that the next step was not to be the university or business but the army, 'the School was pervaded by a curious feeling, almost of careless fatalism,' as Phil MacPherson remembered. For the masters there was the long-drawn-out anguish of the casualty lists. 'At the outbreak of the war,' wrote John Hay Beith, 'there were in existence rather less than 2,000 Fettesians, of whom some 800 or 900 were over 40 years of age. Those who joined up (or were already in the Services) number 1,094. Of that number nearly one quarter – 246 – died for their country, a record of devotion and patriotic duty which can surely be acclaimed, with sorrowful pride, as second to none.' The bravest were often those who had not excelled at school or been the titans of the rugby field. The Anderson brothers had won no athletic distinction at Fettes, and two of them were so frail they were nicknamed 'Crocky'. Yet all four of them – the entire family – died in the field. William, the eldest, was the last to fall, but not before he had won the Victoria Cross. All too often the unnoticed schoolboy turns into the gallant soldier. P. A. Cooper was known as 'Cowpat' at school, where he had excelled at nothing, but in the war he rose rapidly to become Deputy Controller of Trench Warfare, going on afterwards to an immensely distinguished career as Sir Patrick Ashley Cooper,

Deputy Governor of the Hudson's Bay Company and High Sheriff of London.

This small Scottish school was represented on 25 different fronts, and in the Canadian, New Zealand, Australian, South African and Newfoundland Corps as well as the Indian Contingent. Beith records that 'roughly for every ten Fettesians who served in the War, two were awarded decorations and four were Mentioned in Dispatches.' William Anderson and Donald Mackintosh, who fell at the age of 21, won VCs, to add to those already won in 1900 by Matthew Meiklejohn in the Boer War and in 1907 (posthumously) by Hector Maclean. At Fettes, where the young soldiers had so recently been sitting at desks in the form-rooms, the news of each new fatality was awaited with grim resignation. A. W. Hudson, Housemaster in College, had to cope with the fact that, of his nine house prefects in 1914, six were killed and one badly crippled. He became obsessed with the idea that he was a shirker and left Fettes in 1916 to become an ambulance driver on the Italian front.

Donald Mackintosh VC.

The Headmaster, who was already 66 on the outbreak of war, felt it was his duty to stay on and see the School through the War. But in reality he had had enough of schoolmastering, and, worn down by the unrelenting bulletins of the deaths of his boys, he was visibly old and tired. His voice was weak, and his sermons in Chapel could be inaudible and induce sleep. 'I always dread the Sunday night services,' wrote Selwyn Lloyd (the future Chancellor of the Exchequer and Speaker of the House of Commons) to his mother. 'They are so dreadfully boring. The Headmaster always preaches, and Daddy can imagine what it is like.' It was hard to keep up standards, and though Heard's air of authority remained, he seemed ever more distant from the boys. When Richard Humble met him in the corridor wearing his slippers, he mistook him for the head porter. By the time the War came, Heard was unaware of much that was going on in the School. Newcomers could find their lives made a misery by those in their second year, and the fatalism of seniors who knew that to leave school was to go to likely death in the trenches produced a harshness that made this the unhappiest period in the School's history. Games in the houses like obstacle races and dormitory rugger (ferociously contested in a confined space, with 'new men' having to play barefoot, and finally banned in 1917), and a punishment called 'rabbiting' were ordeals for the young and frail. 'To be rabbited,' wrote the young Selwyn Lloyd to his sister, 'is to be chased round the study area by the Prefects with hockey sticks etc.' He did not enjoy his first year in 1918–19.

War meant various shortages. Founder's Day was dropped, along with most entertainments, and the shortage of starch meant soft collars. As lively new recruits to the staff like Alec Ashcroft went off to join their regiments, classes were large. In the kitchens, George Scott the Steward struggled manfully with rationing. For the first two years of the War, the boys' food was little changed, but by 1916 they were going two days a week without meat, and found themselves eating potato bread, with margarine instead of butter. Early-morning cocoa disappeared with the milk shortage, and beer at lunch (for seniors only, and so weak that it was rumoured to have been analysed in the lab and to have failed to answer the test for alcohol) vanished, never to return. The boys were encouraged to grow vegetables in allotments

The Green Walk in June.

on the soccer pitch in an effort to stop their diet becoming drastically unhealthy, and tennis courts were turned into hen-runs. The Sixth Form classicists, who had previously been taught German instead of French so that they could tackle the works of scholars like Ulrich von Wilamowitz-Moellendorf, were diverted from this 'Hunnish language' back to French.

Even so, the War could be kept at arm's length until it forced itself into the consciousness of the boys, as on the evening in 1916 when the first Zeppelins appeared in Edinburgh, and explosions in the Grassmarket and on the Castle Rock sent them scurrying down from their dormitories to huddle in the bottom corridor. In August of the same year, they made a small contribution to the war effort by attending a lumber camp at Pitlochry, where 4,000 to 5,000 trees were cut down to make pit props for the trenches. After the drudgery of sawing and axing, the evenings brought relief in the shape of bathing in the Tummel, eating ice-cream in Pitlochry or (if you had got your parents' permission) the extraordinary licence of legal smoking.

On the whole, though, it was a dour time. The exploits of the rugby and cricket teams provided little real comfort, as key personnel came and went, but at least classical Scholarships at Oxford and Cambridge kept coming as the teaching was strengthened by John Mackay Thomson, who was recruited in 1915 and later became Secretary of the Scottish Education Department. The sensitive Fettesian like Walter Sellar could still find some distraction from the spectre of far-off conflict in the beauty of the School grounds:

> War did not modify the west winds that beat relentlessly on our dormitory skylights, nor dim the blaze of hawthorn and laburnum along the Green Walk in June; among

50

the shadows the blackbirds and greenfinches went about their business. At the western end of the Below Fields, when the whistles blew for 'No-side' at half-past three, the winter sun was a red disc glowing among the pines; and, late in summer evenings, when pale skies lay low across the hills of Fife, there was a shimmer among the willows by the pond. Such beauty, for all the unearthly silence of it, makes surely its loud appeal to heart and memory.

The end came quite suddenly, as a babel of sirens and whistles announced the Armistice on the morning of 11th November 1918. 'It was a queer, breathless moment,' wrote Robert Hardie, later to spend much of the Second War on the Burma Railway. Phil Macpherson remembered the whole School going to the front of College after lunch 'to send cheer after ringing cheer into the frosty air.' A few days later the School was taken out in steamers to cruise round the surrendered German ships lying in the Forth (soon to scuttle themselves at Scapa Flow). 'The Huns seemed very happy and contented,' said *The Fettesian*, somewhat optimistically. 'It was a rather horrible performance' was Hardie's verdict.

Heard had already launched the scheme for a Fettes War Memorial in 1917. This raised over £20,000, to be used for erecting a Memorial in the grounds, and helping Fettesians who had suffered in the War.

At the end of the first summer term after the War, Dr Heard retired. The first Founder's Day for five years, held in May 1919, was his farewell. In his speech, Heard talked of the War, and of six Heads of School who had fallen in succession in the trenches of Flanders. He himself had by now served the School for 44 years, nearly 30 of them as Headmaster, and he compared himself to the 'harmless, necessary cab-horse, which noble animal has, at last, had to relinquish all hopes of winning the Derby.' He was now 70. By seeing the School through the War, he had perhaps hastened his own death. A poem in *The Fettesian* wished him 'the lingering sweetness of the setting sun, the golden evening hours that whisper "Peace",' but he was in fact to live for less than two more years. As with Potts before him, his sense of duty ruled much of what he did. Between them they had covered almost the first 50 years of the School's existence.

Heard was the longest-serving of all Fettes headmasters, and in the end stayed too long. But he had dedicated most of his working life to the School and kept up numbers, so that his successor took over a school of 235 boys. His classical teaching had ensured that the academic momentum created by Potts was not lost, and he had brought the School through, ready for a new, post-war beginning under a much younger man. Of the ideal Headmaster, Ian Hay, who served under Heard, wrote: 'Such a man is Olympian, having none of the foibles or soft moments of a human being. He dwells apart, in an atmosphere too rarefied for those who intrude into it.' Heard had been respected rather than loved by his colleagues and boys, and it is hard to know what effect his wife's very early death had on a naturally reticent temperament. But in retrospect Walter Sellar was able to write of him: 'There is an almost unanimous opinion amongst those who knew Dr Heard best that he was something more than a great Headmaster; that he was, potentially at least, a "Great Man".'

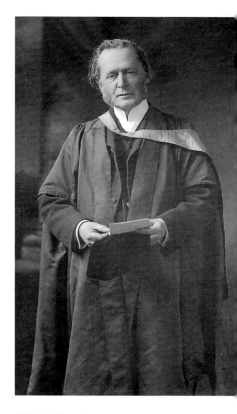

W. A. Heard, 1919.

Remembrance Day Service.

4

The Classical Continuum
ASHCROFT : 1919–45

After Heard's 30-year reign, the Governors wanted a new broom, but not a radical change in the system. Rugby, Classics and undogmatic Christianity were the three pillars of Fettes life, and in 1914 the School had waved off to the trenches a young man who united all three. He was now back from the Front, looking for the right post. Of the 12 applicants for the vacant headship, he was the only one interviewed.

Alec Ashcroft was a Cambridge rugby Blue and an England cap, a double First in Classics and history and a committed Methodist (known at Cambridge as 'the wealthy Wesleyan'). After Birkenhead School and Caius College, Cambridge, he had come to teach at Fettes between 1910 and 1914, where he had been known in the (mainly 40-plus) Common Room as 'The Babe'. He had had an impressive war. He became a Major and was mentioned three times in Dispatches, achieving a DSO and the Order of the Crown of Italy.

With the arrival in 1919 of this 32-year-old war hero, a gust of fresh air blew into the School. He replaced a man who was his senior by 38 years. The decline in numbers during the War had not been dramatic, but life had become too spartan and barbaric, and Ashcroft poured his energy into the pursuit of humanity and comfort. First he had to finalise the plans for a War Memorial. By November, these had reached the stage where a full-scale model of Burnie Rhind's design was put experimentally in front of College. The figure of a kilted, dying soldier, right arm upraised in a terminal gesture of defiance over the inscription 'Carry On', was felt to be dramatic and eloquent. When the model was moved to the east, though, everyone agreed it looked better there. The Memorial has dominated the main approach to College up the East Drive ever since, and been the annual setting for Remembrance Sunday services. The solemn autumnal atmosphere on these Sundays is something often recalled by Fettesians, the whole School clustered round the Memorial, the backdrop of the misty Edinburgh skyline and the silence broken by the distant boom of the Castle gun and the skirling of 'The Flowers of the Forest' drifting up from the unseen piper below.

Meanwhile, Ashcroft vigorously set about improving the quality of life. He started on food and warmth. In the War, Fettesians had often been cold and

Alec Ashcroft on his arrival at Fettes.

53

General Sir William Macpherson, OF, at the unveiling of the War Memorial, with the inscription 'Carry On', by Burnie Rhind.

Dr Andrew Flett, the kindly School doctor, with his Rolls.

hungry. David Ogilvy, however, arriving in 1924, found that 'Fettes provided delicious Scottish porridge, three times a day, and Scottish roast beef, and Scottish mutton pies. For the next five years I lived like a fighting cock.' In his first year Ashcroft asked 'Johnnie' Coast to organise the conversion of the old wooden sickhouse into a tuck-shop, stocking forgotten luxuries like Nice, Bourbon and Café Noir biscuits, chocolate, fruit and a mysterious lemony liquid called Zetrils. Warmth at long last spread through College when a central heating system was installed in the autumn of 1920. It operated by steam. When it was first introduced into the protesting pipes, Robert Hardie wrote, 'there seemed hardly a moment in which the radiators were not misbehaving in some way, with obstreperous hissings and gurglings, or sudden loud and quite inexplicable clanks and clangs.' It settled down with time, but the clanks and clangs are still a phenomenon today, at odd, inopportune moments. The health of the boys was in good hands when in 1923 Ashcroft hired Andrew Flett as School doctor. Flett drove a Rolls and got on with everyone. His remedy for a young staff wife suffering from post-natal depression was a case of champagne with a note prescribing a couple of glasses each evening. The Sanatorium (to which you were taken if ill enough in a sedan chair called 'the death cart') was presided over by Miss Carruthers who 'on arrival handed you a beaker of castor oil with no regard for the nature of your illness,' wrote David Ogilvy. 'However, when I was admitted with rheumatic fever, this dear dragon saved my life by her gentle nursing.'

The drive to civilise the community went on. There was a new feeling in the air, and 'life,' wrote Robert Hardie, 'became brighter and freer.' Ashcroft had no time for the bullying and sexual experimentation which seemed so inevitable a feature of boarding schools. He was helped by prefects like Selwyn Lloyd, determined that his own unhappy time as a new arrival should not be endured by others. The inhumanity of boy to boy could not be banished at a stroke, but Ashcroft consciously dispensed a gentler ethos. Tanqueray of Moredun seems to have been the only housemaster who thought of giving his boys any sort of sex instruction. The bad experiences of Selwyn Lloyd and Michael Tippett in their first year had reflected the lax standards of the late War years, but by the late 1920s, wrote Ian Harvey in *To Fall like Lucifer*, 'the fact is that homosexual practice was almost non-existent, compared with what one has heard of other schools.' This is confirmed for the 1930s by Sir Roderick Macdonald (in *The Scottish Review*, July 1995). Everything was too public for such activities. 'An "unnatural" offence at Fettes would have led to a short conversation in the Headmaster's study swiftly followed by a taxi with luggage to the station.' Not that any effort was made to provide female distraction. 'Female employees were clearly vetted with a view to safety rather than pulchritude. A busty wee lass was once through an oversight employed as a house laundry maid. She lasted one day, creating a traffic jam for button replacements.' Rugby still dominated the atmosphere, though excesses of fervour like 'battle hymns' before key fixtures were curbed by Ashcroft, while the local press was asked to be less hyperbolic in the way it reported school matches. A traditionalist like Robert Bruce Lockhart saw this 'damping-down process' as resulting in a fall in the number of

The old tuck shop.

'Nunky' Brown, the first leader of the Fettesian-Lorettonian Boys' Club. Cartoon by Tom Curr.

Fettesians winning Blues or Scottish caps. 'I sometimes wonder,' he mused, 'if the new graces have been acquired at the cost of a certain lack of virility.'

Ashcroft soon had Kimmerghame House (closed during the War) reopened under the gentle Henry Cooke (whose wife Theresa was Ashcroft's sister-in-law). Young, vigorous new masters were signed up, and Ashcroft laid plans for injecting life into music and drama. Debating was encouraged under Walter Sellar and, later, Geoffrey Sale, and helped future politicians like Ian Harvey and Iain MacLeod to develop the cut and thrust of argument. Ashcroft projected an ideal of service of which he was himself the best example. The boys were to put more into the community than they took out of it. His dedication was total. To his pupils work became 'a thing of living and human interest', and he was so involved in the rugby that, as well as coaching the 1st XV, he played on Bigside himself until he dislocated his shoulder in November 1921. He had a fine record to keep up. Until 1920, Fettes had played school matches only against Loretto, Merchiston, the Edinburgh Academy and Glenalmond, but of the total of 227 matches played, 155 had been won.

The drive for improvement continued in 1924 when electric light was put in. In the same year the partnership with Loretto was cemented when the Fettesian-Lorettonian Boys' Club opened just off the High Street, 'to win (its members) from the dubious pleasures of the streets,' as Ian Hay put it. It was a timely move with the days of the Depression looming. It was given a fine start by the appointment of Hewitson ('Nunky') Brown as its first club leader. This unique man, wrote Knox Cunningham, 'was the catalytic agent who influenced the lives of countless Fettesians, Lorettonians and club members.' In 1925 H. T. Young gave money to lay out and develop the northernmost part of the grounds (close to Ferry Road) as extra games pitches, to be known as Young's Field. In the same year gravel was laid

*Fettesian-Lorettonian Boys'
Club boys taking baths in sinks.*

*Harry Pyatt, the Housemaster of
Carrington, with his wife,
Fanny.*

down in immense quantities up the East and West Drives and all round the College buildings, where the 1870 gravel had more or less disappeared. It was laid so deep that progress across it was like walking in glue. On Founder's Day the 'Vive-La' contained the verse:

> Now I rather expect you'll have noticed the gravel,
> And have found it perhaps a slight hindrance to travel.
> I'll give you a tip, if it's progress you lack.
> When I want to go forwards, I always go back.

Of Ashcroft's new appointments, one made a crucial impact on the aesthetic life of the place. When Henry Havergal (later to be Principal of the Scottish Academy of Music) was signed up as Director of Music in 1924, he elevated music at a stroke from a Cinderella subject to a source of real pride for the School. Music had been taught from the start by a series of sound practitioners like A. W. Dace, who spent a remarkable 51 years at the School. But what happened now was that music became fashionable. Muscular rugby players who in the past had regarded flautists or singers as irretrievably unmanly were suddenly begging to join the choir – even bad singers, who were sometimes told by Havergal 'Come in but keep quiet!' The record library he started meant that a non-performer like Ian Hunter could still pick up the love of music that was to lead him later on to become the first Artistic Director of the Edinburgh Festival.

It was a help to Havergal when masters joined in the music-making, like Harry Pyatt, Housemaster of Carrington, who gave concerts the spice of eccentricity. So absent-minded was he that three school prefects were enlisted before a concert, one to get Pyatt to the Concert Hall, the second his music, the third his double bass. Even when all three were successfully reassembled in the Hall, it wasn't all plain sailing. Once when an unusually weird sound was heard, it turned out he'd been given the flute part and was doggedly trying to play it on his double bass. On another he caught his bow in a string and it was catapulted over people's heads to the corner of the Hall. On a third, a concert scheduled to start with a double bass note began thus:

1. Conductor brings down baton.
2. The bow of Pyatt's double bass snaps with a loud crack.
3. Pyatt (*sotto voce*, audible to all): 'Damn!'

When Ashcroft came, Pyatt had served 15 years in Carrington. This was in fact quite enough, but Ashcroft let him stay another 15 before retiring in 1935 (just as he let Tanqueray stay for 31 years until he was 70, depriving younger masters of any chance of promotion). After Pyatt's controversial appointment in 1905, he had worked his way gradually into the affections of his boys who at first thought him insufficiently rugged. But, though he inspired loyalty, he was much too vague about what was going on to be a successful housemaster. A poet and intellectual, Pyatt was something unique in the cultural mix of the School. He did not hold mainstream Fettes views. 'Rugby is a game for louts and bullies,' he declared. 'Cricket is a waste of time.' 'The presence of a poet, utterly vague and infinitely humane,' wrote George Morrison, 'was a blessing indeed.' The really clever, sensitive boys found his classes exciting. In his Latin lessons, visual aids might include a fat cartoon Horace on the blackboard, ensconced in a deck chair under an arbutus tree, puffing a cigar and holding a Falernian and soda. There were snags, though. His fly buttons would often be undone ('I see no opening for mirth,' he would say as the boys giggled) and sometimes there would be long silences as he gazed out of the window. He had forgotten the class was there. In Carrington he was a delightful host, helped by his wife Fanny, but on one occasion, as he lifted the lid of the teapot to stir, a mushy mass could be seen. 'Hullo!' said Pyatt. 'There's my cheque book.'

As the decade wore on towards the General Strike in 1926, political apathy ruled in the School, though the boys were certain that Arthur Cook, the miners' leader, was the villain of the piece and that Fettesian Lord Simon's speech on 6th May was what brought it to an end. In the summer of that year, the Golf Course that had been laid out between the 'Jordan' and Young's field was opened with a match between masters and boys. R. R. MacGibbon, Head of School, was the first off the tee and struck his ball out of bounds, but his recovery was so remarkable that he was credited with a two! In the following year, the first phase of Ashcroft's development programme was completed with the opening in the south-west corner of the grounds of the new Kimmerghame House. It was lighter and roomier than any of the other houses, and was the only 'outhouse' to have central heating. After 47 years of existence as a house of 12–15 boys, it was at last on a par with the rest, though it kept its individual character from those years.

With the end of the 1930s Ashcroft could look back on his first decade with no little satisfaction. Fettes life had not fundamentally changed, and it was, wrote Ian More, 'a great Scots public school which still clung to much of its sternness of hard living, rugger and Classics.' But a continual series of material improvements had made life easier for the ordinary boy, and school numbers stood at 270, the highest yet. The rugby XV was still successful and everyone was able to take pride in the exploits of the three Fettesians playing for Scotland: Phil Macpherson as Captain,

A caricature of Harry Pyatt.

Aerial view of the School estate in 1929, showing the newly-built Kimmerghame House at the bottom of the picture.

David MacMyn and Herbert Waddell, whom the boys watched winning the 1930 match against Wales with a late drop goal to take Scotland's first Grand Slam. The games menu now included squash, and the new courts built in 1930 were the first in Scotland. Ashcroft's teaching of the Latin and Greek authors was inspirational and enlivened by constant parallels with the modern day. It produced impressive results after the groundwork had been done by fine teachers like Pyatt, Freddy Macdonald and Carl Edgar Young. Macdonald (the only Scot on the staff) had arrived in 1925 as K. P. Wilson left. Since 'K. P.' had arrived in 1884 and Freddy Macdonald was not to retire until 1962, these two Fettes stalwarts covered between them 78 years of the School's history. Everyone was amazed at Freddy's energy when he arrived from Oxford, and he held forth with equal conviction on *Oratio Obliqua* or rucking technique, playing the organ in Chapel and giving up his spare time to extra coaching. He was, remembered Roddy Macdonald, 'the only completely good man' he had ever met. Carl Edgar Young was a talented classicist and something of a *bon viveur*, apt to bet large sums on horses until he married the daughter of a Bishop, settled down and finally became Headmaster of Rossall and a Canon. There were talented non-classicists around, too. Daniel Vawdrey was one of the few who could really appeal to the non-academic boys with his battery of learning aids, and he was, thought Donald Crichton-Miller, the first to bridge the gap between boys and masters. He usually started his classes with the words, 'Well, gents.' In the 1920s the Upper Mods were taught history by Walter Sellar. The famous dictum found in his book *1066 and All That*, 'History is not what happened. It is what you can remember,' perhaps reflects the strategies he adopted in getting the Mods to learn.

Punishment was sensibly administered under Ashcroft, though 'Pow' Edwards

The epitome of the public school boy all-rounder, R. R. MacGibbon, Head of School (who played the opening match on the Golf Course, 1926). At Oxford he was a rugby Blue (twice) and was awarded a First in Greats.

Henry Cotton opening the new Golf Course, 1952. The old course had been ploughed up during the War for cereal crops.

was felt to be excessive in his use of the slipper and the cane. Divisions between years were still deep, and Cameron Miller, ill in the Sanatorium in 1927, found the other patient in his room was Alan Scroggie, his senior by two years. It was not until Scroggie saw fit to say 'Good morning,' on the third day that they could begin a conversation. There was little class feeling within the School, however. Few, if any boys came from big landed families, but in any case Fettesians showed little interest in what each other's parents did. In most respects the Fettes of the 1930s was a self-confident, happy school. Graham Richardson, arriving in 1935 to teach modern languages, found it 'a very hard working and hard playing school at every level.' He was amazed at what housemasters thought of as normal and at their devotion to their boys. The bachelors' Common Room was a cheerful place, filled with talented young men like Wilfred Hoare, Geoffrey Sale, Idwal Rees, Dick Evers, Terence Jones, Hugh Elder and, later, Dick Cole-Hamilton, Tommy Evans and Dick Knight. Ashcroft was adept at appointing good staff, and 12 of them ended up as headmasters elsewhere. Rossall and Strathallan each took two in succession. Men who stayed on, like the loyal Gwynne Newman, provided continuity and stability. The happiness of the Common Room was instrumental in the way it functioned as a unit, and this *esprit de corps* was to continue to be one of the School's key strengths. It is easy to over-emphasise the role of masters in the life of the School, however, since for the rank and file the senior boys were a far more immediate agent of authority. Many of the houses (like the games) were virtually run by the prefects.

The ease with which the 1930s appear in retrospect a time of seething tension and underlying gloom is belied by the apparent serenity with which they passed inside the School's red railings. 'What memory recalls,' wrote George Morrison, 'is a series of quiet years which may indeed have borne a close resemblance to that other halcyon period forever lost, the years before 1914.' The School was 'suspended in a time-warp between two World Wars, and not a cloud on the horizon,' wrote Roddy Macdonald. Military feelings rarely surfaced, though 'it was perhaps at OTC Camp that the black cloud of disaster loomed most heavily upon the little world of school, as the fresh wind of the Fifeshire coast rustled the flaps of the marquee where, in the stuffy, canvas-smelling shade, a bemedalled officer in tartan trews pointed with his cane to the latest infantry weapon, the new Czech Bren gun. But after a sunlit afternoon spent swimming by the seaweed-encrusted rocks, the shadow had disappeared.'

Edwards was now the doyen of the staff, having been at the School for over 30 years. 'Bald and bucolic, with piercing piggy eyes and a stinging rapier wit', he was a successful Housemaster of Glencorse. He had an incisive mind, and was once introduced by Lodge as a 'shining example of the principle that hair won't grow on top of brains.' He was not a man to cross swords lightly with in debate. Some called him 'Ho', since this word so often prefaced his statements, as in (to boy baffled by question) 'Ho, gracious! Interval for deep thought,' or (to colleague venturing an opinion) 'Ho, I didn't believe any thinking man thought *that* nowadays.' A good teacher of bright mathematicians, he tended to apply his subject in all situations, as

Tug of war.

Programme for the Scotland v. England match at Murrayfield, 21st March 1925. The Scottish team contained three OFs, all of whom signed the programme.

when one day in summer someone hit a cricket ball in the air and shouted 'Heads!' Everyone ducked except Edwards, who had speedily calculated the odds of it landing on his head as infinitesimal. It was a day of long odds, however, and it scored a direct hit on his straw hat. Edwards' biting tongue meant that class discipline was no problem for him, and he was apparently the original of Mr Wellings in *The Lighter Side of School Life*, who 'ruled entirely by the lash of his tongue. A schoolboy can put up with stripes, and he rather relishes abuse; but sarcasm withers him to the marrow.'

The man who had taken over Carrington from Pyatt in 1935, however, was larger than life – 'king of hyperbole,' wrote Graham Richardson, 'faintly redolent of Tartarin de Tarascon and Baron Münchausen.' Wilfred ('Jerry') Lodge had arrived to teach Physics at the age of 28, straight from commanding a battalion of the Royal Scots. Finding suitable science teachers was always hard. In his book *The Housemaster*, Ian Hay wrote of Dr Adams that he 'had once lamented at a masters' meeting the impossibility of procuring a science master who was a gentleman.' In Lodge, Ashcroft found one who was a gentleman. But although a good scientist himself, he was quite unable to get down to his pupils' level. His lessons tended to consist of five minutes' talk, after which he either gave the class ten examples to do and left, or else read aloud from a novel. 'The boy's an imbecile,' he said of one pupil. 'I spent five whole minutes explaining logarithms and he still doesn't understand them.' He was one of the great housemasters, though. His language was all too often politically incorrect, but between him and his boys there was, said John Blelloch, 'a trust and respect that really was mutual,' and in the late 1930s, with a series of future headmasters as his house tutors and his resourceful house man Joe McArthur, the house was the envy of the School.

Lodge knew his boys and they appreciated his wisdom as well as his sheer panache. He was a distinctive figure as he moved round the grounds, 6' 7" tall and immaculate in black coat with Astrakhan collar, black Homburg and grey buttoned spats. He dominated his House, knowing when and when not to intervene in the régime of the prefects (a delicate area for any housemaster). Commanding the absolute loyalty of his boys, he could afford to be dismissive of their parents. 'Mr. Lodge, Mr. Lodge!' cried one Carrington mother who had arrived out of the blue one Sunday morning. 'I've just been to my son's study and it isn't fit for a pig to live in.' 'It may not be fit for a pig to live in,' riposted Lodge, 'but it is certainly good enough for your son.' He had a strong idea of good form. When, after a game of golf at Gullane, his younger colleagues put a feather in his hat as a joke, he disowned it. 'Couldn't be seen dead in it,' he reported, 'so I took a taxi home.' Travelling hatless by public transport was impossibly bad form.

Ashcroft, by contrast, presided over the Common Room and the School in the most unassuming way possible. He was in no sense a grand figure, but his honesty, modesty, kindness and undisguised concern for the good of his school inspired the warmest loyalty. In 1938 his qualities were recognised by the award of an honorary LL.D from St Andrews, though he typically treated this as an honour to the whole School. He was a superlative teacher ('You lived what he taught,' said Tommy

J. S. Edwards in his cricket gear, 1923.

Wilfred 'Jerry' Lodge when he left in 1948.

Macpherson), and overall a total of 94 of his pupils gained open classical awards at Oxford or Cambridge. This record far outdistanced that of any other Scottish public school of the time. He was less good as an administrator, and his greatest weakness was a failure in curriculum development. He was quite ignorant of science. 'He expounded the *De Rerum Natura* of Lucretius,' wrote David Grant, 'as if it were the last word on its subject.' He was so committed to his beloved Classics that he could barely conceive that other respectable avenues to academic distinction existed.

By the mid-1930s the brilliant achievements of his pupils could not disguise the fact that his curriculum was slipping out of date, and his failure to open it up to science and modern languages and adapt it to the needs of the weaker academics was starting to lose the School custom. The numbers started to decline, from 270 in 1935 to a low of 166 in 1942. This was not unusual in the aftermath of the depression, but the Headmaster of nearby Cargilfield Prep School, 'Rufus' Bruce Lockhart, was a linguist and saw the Fettes classical monopoly as narrow and *passé*. He had some influence with other prep school headmasters, and when in 1936 he went as Headmaster to Sedbergh, he took many Scottish boys with him. None of this helped Fettes, and Ashcroft's aversion to PR was an extra factor. This probably had its roots in his natural conservatism and tendency to self-effacement. Early on, he had urged the local papers to moderate the extraordinary excesses of their rugby reports and not mention individual Fettes players by name. When in 1925 a Fettes party went up Mont Blanc (singing a verse of 'Floreas Fettesia' at the top) and was rewarded with pictures and an account of the climb in a local paper, Ashcroft's view

Alec Ashcroft.

Cricket on Below Fields, painting by William Wilson, 1945.

was clear: such publicity was vulgar.

Upgrading of the buildings continued in the late 1930s, though there was less spare cash available. One by one, the boarding houses had their changing-rooms and bathrooms overhauled. In 1938, a decision was taken to build a new hall (to house concerts, assembly and Chapel) to the west of College and make the old Chapel into a fine new library. As war loomed in 1939, the plan was dropped, never to be resurrected. Until 1953, a fragment of a specimen wall stood by what is now West Woods as a forlorn monument to what might have been.

As the year 1939 wore on and the writing could be read ever more clearly on the wall, six bomb-proof shelters were excavated out of the grassy slopes in front of College. Unpalatable demands from the authorities followed, including a threatened requisition order on *all* the school buildings and a request for the School's iron railings to be handed over for scrap. Ashcroft had visions of uncontrolled marauding over the grounds if the iron perimeter barrier went, but he was saved by a military veto when it turned out the Home Guard had earmarked Fettes, with its barricade of railings, as a strong point if Scotland were invaded.

Within a month of the outbreak of war in October 1939, the School had a rare close-up view of hostilities, with the first air raid of the War, the only *Luftwaffe* strike on Rosyth Naval Base. Jack Mackenzie Stuart was playing in a House Below on 16th October on the south-west corner of the playing fields: 'The ball had emerged from the loose scrum and one of the centres kicked ahead to the east. The forwards followed up making for the opposing full-back who stood facing west ready to gather the ball. Suddenly his expression changed to one of complete astonishment and the ball sailed unnoticed over his shoulder.' He had seen a Junkers 88 bomber coming straight towards him at less than 1,000 ft, with smoke pouring out of an engine. It was being chased by two Spitfires. They might have brought it down in the School grounds, but the pilots courteously stopped firing over the playing fields (perhaps because one of them was Old Fettesian George Denholm), finally forcing it down in the sea off Port Seton. Another was shot down off Crail, in Fife. No sirens were yet operational in Edinburgh, and locals like Alexia Lindsay

The Mont Blanc expedition reaches its goal, 1925. The party included Donald Crichton-Miller and J. M. Scott, who later became a distinguished explorer.

The proposed new Chapel and Concert Hall, work on which was abandoned in 1939, never to be resumed.

Boys digging trenches, September 1938. The Autumn term of that year began in the middle of the Munich Crisis. It was clear that a blitzkrieg might be imminent, so senior boys and masters dug trenches in front of the College. The crisis ended but the danger did not pass, so the Governors decided to erect air-raid shelters and to keep the School in its existing situation rather than to move to Floors Castle, which was offered to them, but which had no facilities.

and her sister, who had heard that the RAF would be practising that day, waved merrily at the planes. The pilot of one German plane that got away reported back home that the Scottish peasants, clearly disaffected, had waved sympathetically at them. This was the first of a notable number of strikes by Denholm, who ended up with a DFC.

Kimmerghame was taken over in 1940 for the duration of the War by the Royal Navy to house the mine research unit HMS *Vernon*. Its boys reluctantly transferred from their fine modern house to Glencorse, where Geoffrey Sale took over as Wilfred Hoare left to join the army. This at least meant that the overheads of one house were being covered by the Navy, which made economic sense, as numbers were down anyway. They reached a low of 166 in 1942. Prospective parents seem to have been worried that the School's location in a capital city on the east coast near Rosyth Naval Base made it vulnerable to bombing. In 1943 and 1944, however, as Edinburgh suffered remarkably little, confidence came back and numbers rose again. The important thing was that, by contrast with the First World War, morale remained high, and the wartime school was a united, happy place. Mrs Scott found the boys 'at all times very co-operative and always willing to do their bit.' Everyone on the staff was overworking, and Ashcroft went back (at the age of 53) to coaching the 1st XV with Freddy Macdonald. The last side he coached (Cuthbertson's XV) was one of the best ever. Self-denial came naturally to him, and Graham Richardson, taking problems to him in his Lodge of an evening, would find him and his wife Betty sitting in overcoats and rugs in front of an empty grate. He used to dig Miss Crawford's garden for her in Malcolm House, and even gave up weeks of his summer holiday to helping with harvest camps at Ceres in Fife. There he did the most menial jobs like sweeping floors and scrubbing tables, while the boys were bringing in sugar-beet or spreading muck. The village parties given for them provided moments of relaxation, of a non-schoolmasterly sort. Ashcroft came back from one red-faced after experiencing the enthusiasm of the Fife girls for Postman's Knock.

George Denholm, the OF Spitfire pilot who in 1939 achieved one of many notable strikes against the Luftwaffe after chasing a Junkers 88 over the College grounds, considerately refraining from firing as he did so.

Dick Evers, on the staff between 1932 and 1940, who captained the Scottish hockey team and who was killed in North Africa in 1943.

With over 1,000 Old Fettesians on active service, more than 170 received decorations and over 130 were mentioned in dispatches. One hundred and eighteen died, 'a grievous total,' said Ashcroft, 'in a war that did not take so heavy a toll of life as did the War 1914–18.' Dick Evers, Fettes master and son of a Fettes master, scholar, athlete and musician, fell in the deserts of North Africa. Of the four Nimmo brothers who served (winning between them one DSO, two MCs and a mention) three were killed, as were two of the three Gallie brothers. Sandy Hodge won the George Cross for remarkable heroism during a ship-board explosion. There were intriguing encounters in different theatres of war. Nick Hammond (destined to become an eminent Greek historian) and Jock Hamilton met in a cave on Crete leading different groups of Greek partisans. Earlier on, Hamilton was inspecting a group of new prisoners in camp one day when he recognised the Italian ice-cream seller who had run a stall on the touch-line of Bigside at rugby matches in his schooldays. He made him Camp Steward. In the POW camp at Chieti, a reunion photograph was taken when it was discovered that every house at Fettes was represented. Peter Allsebrook and David Mitchell escaped together from POW camp in Italy, disguised themselves as Italian workmen and proceeded to apply for jobs in the local German garrison. Peter was finally singled out to be personal servant to the CO, whose last words to him, when the Germans finally had to retreat, were: 'If only all Italians were as efficient as you, we wouldn't be losing this bloody war.'

No Fettes boy had such a traumatic time as Charles Herzberg. His parents had moved from Austria to Britain in the 1930s, but after a short time in Kimmerghame at the start of the war, he was suddenly interned without warning as a German national. His records then got mixed up and he found himself in a shipload of prisoners of war on the way to Canada. There at Red Rock, in the northernmost part of the Great Lakes, they chopped down trees and laid pipes for a paper factory in temperatures that went down to –40 °C. The savage conditions were made worse by Charles' realisation that nobody knew where he was. The Chairman of the Governors had tried to find him, but it was not until his father, who had been told he was lost at sea, told the general manager of Canadian Pacific (who passed the message on to his agents) that the wheels started to turn. One agent was drinking in a bar at Port Arthur, Lake Superior and happened to meet one of the soldiers who were guarding the Red Rock prisoners. After a painfully extended homecoming, Charles at long last appeared back at Kimmerghame a year later. After one and a half years of cramming, he got into Cambridge.

The War brought two crucial changes in the boys' attitudes. The rigid barriers between different years at long last started to come down. The crises of war did something that the mere passage of years had not. As boys of every age huddled together in the air-raid shelters, sharing the same fear and discomfort, the older boys couldn't help feeling 'more avuncular and less disposed to tyrannise.' The other change was that they became less introspective. Jack Mackenzie Stuart felt that in 1939 'the red railings surrounding the grounds . . . shut out the exterior world.' Even the cinema was out of bounds, and wireless sets were forbidden (though illegal crystal sets were used to hear key broadcasts like the Abdication speech). The little world within the railings could too easily seem all-sufficient, but the War started the process of breaking this barrier down. It was a happy, united, tolerant time.

When Ashcroft could see the end clearly in sight late in 1944, he decided to resign. He would still be only 58, two years short of the statutory limit, but he knew several large public schools would be in the market for post-war headmasters, and he wanted Fettes to strike early. Perhaps he remembered that his predecessor had stayed on too long for the good of the School. He could see the changes that lay ahead and wanted a new man to launch them and see them through. The Governors reluctantly accepted his resignation.

Ashcroft's departure in 1945 marked a watershed in the School's history. For the first 75 years of its existence it had been presided over by three Headmasters only, of whom the second and third were former members of the Fettes staff. All three were unworldly Classicists motivated by firm religious belief and a sense of duty. The unusual continuity this produced had brought brilliant academic and rugby results, a hardy life-style and a powerful sense of purpose which had sustained the School's self-belief. But the continuity had bred conservatism, and many fundamentals had changed little in the 75 years. The popularity which had come to the School with its obvious excellence in the Classics and on the games field was finally being eroded by a perceived failure to keep up with the pace of curricular advance. All three Heads had looked down on the very non-classical subjects which were now crowding in, pressing for attention. Numbers had recovered to 213 from the 1942 low, but the School's capacity was now 270, and firm action was needed to recapture the market.

Ashcroft's dedication and unselfishness meant that, though few boys knew him really well, those who did had a deep affection for him. No-one could call a man grasping whose salary in 1945 was £1,000 (plus capitation), the same as that earned by Potts in 1870 (inflation zero over 75 years). He had no secretary and wrote all his letters in his own hand. He passed on to his successor healthy finances and sound fabric in spite of the ravages of war. In many ways his Headship was a golden time. After his last assembly in July 1945, he stood outside at the top of the stairs in College and shook hands with every boy in the School. A third former like Jock Smith was amazed to see that there were tears in the eyes of this self-effacing man he hardly knew. Ashcroft was deeply fond of the School to which he had given so much of his life, and to him, as with Potts, duty was all.

Fettes 'reunion' at the POW camp in Chieti, Italy, in 1943. A couple of days after this was taken, two of them escaped.

Founder's Day tea, 29th July 1946.

5

Expansion
CRICHTON-MILLER : 1945–58

As peace arrived with the summer of 1945, Fettes emerged into a new era. Not all the Governors wanted radical change, and the Chairman, Lord Normand, was keen for another classicist to be appointed in Ashcroft's place to sustain the School's position as the premier classical school of Scotland. Ashcroft suggested OF Nick Hammond (later to be Professor of Greek at Bristol and Headmaster of Clifton), but he was still serving in Greece and though Normand sent 'various coded Homeric messages' out to him it was to no avail. When his fellow-Governors cast their votes for Donald Crichton-Miller, Normand resigned soon afterwards. Crichton-Miller's appointment as Headmaster did not just mean the end of the 75-year dominance of the Classics, it directed a searchlight into every area of school life. He was not a former Fettes master like his two predecessors, but he was the son of a Fettesian and had been at Fettes himself. This link was to prove no obstacle to drastic reform of his *alma mater*.

A boy at Fettes between 1920 and 1925, Crichton-Miller was Head of School and won an Exhibition in history (then a rare event) to Pembroke College, Cambridge. There he was awarded his Blue for rugby and went on to gain three caps for Scotland. He taught in turn at Monmouth, Bryanston and Stowe, where he learnt from its remarkable Headmaster J. F. Roxburgh the 'expansiveness of manner' he was to exhibit at Taunton, where he became Headmaster in 1936 at the age of 29. He was 38 when he arrived at Fettes. At his first assembly a month after VJ Day, he told the boys they would get an extra half-day a week. The ones who thought this meant more spare time were soon disabused. But they sat up. Their new Head clearly meant business, and the notice on his study door – 'Come in, don't knock' – suggested that he wanted to get to know them. His habit of saying exactly what he thought was disconcerting, and he could give an impression of *hauteur* and even arrogance, but he was fair, had a good sense of humour and (crucially) knew everything that was going on. The boys were to discover that he was liable to pop up all over the place. He might appear unannounced in the 'spray-room' of one of the boarding houses because he had an inkling there was some bullying going on there. 'At any turn you might meet him, wearing his white

Donald Crichton-Miller as a young man.

67

The precarious-looking galleries put up in the Chapel by Crichton-Miller to increase its capacity.

duffle-coat,' remembered Francis Pearson. His presence often made people feel guilty, but it galvanized them. 'Whenever I see him looking at me,' said Geoffrey Sale, 'I feel I should be somewhere else, doing something else, twice as quickly.'

Crichton-Miller was at heart a businessman. He had already decided the School needed four things – more boys, a broader curriculum, more up-to-date facilities, and a wider choice of games and activities. War-time inflation was already putting pressure on the School's economy from rising costs of maintenance and salaries, and in order to make sure the books balanced, he soon brought up from Taunton the excellent Harold Bond to take over the accounts. If fees were not to go through the roof, a rise in school numbers seemed the only answer. It would not be simple. The School's buildings could not easily be expanded without massive capital outlay, and care had to be taken that rising numbers did not destroy the intimacy of the boarding atmosphere.

Crichton-Miller, however, did not agonize for long. It was a case, he said later, of 'expand or perish', and in any case, raising numbers was for him what constituted success. Years afterwards he was to tell Bob Roberts, then Headmaster of Worksop: 'You'll be judged, old boy, by only one thing: whether or not you're a getter of boys.' He moved with relish to cash in on the post-war seller's market. In his first year, school numbers stood at 223, but by the end of the 1946 summer holiday the figure had risen to 311. Kimmerghame House, which had been closed to boys during the War and was built to take 49, reopened with 64 boys, later to rise to 76. Immediate steps had to be taken elsewhere to cope with the surge in numbers, and first of all a division was made into Upper and Lower School. Chapel and meals could now be run in two sessions, and class-room capacity was increased by partitioning the big class-rooms at each end of the College building. More was achieved by adaptation than by new buildings. Once (remembered John Robson) after Crichton-Miller with others was invited to see round a warship, he remarked as they came ashore: 'You know, old boy, these chaps have a lot to teach us about space management.' 'What next?' thought the others. 'Hammocks slung above beds?' When in 1948 dry rot was discovered in the Chapel, the chance was taken to add a chancel and gallery, so that the whole School could again be fitted in. The Chapel's location on the first floor made extensions as such impossible (hence the abortive plans for a new Chapel in 1890 and again in 1938). At the time the new chancel seemed the only option to provide room for more boys, but the way it spoilt Bryce's external roof line has offended the eye ever since. As Crichton-Miller drove the numbers up above 400 by 1952, a second, vertiginous gallery was to be added in 1955 and a gallery squeezed into the Chancel for those less than 5' 5" tall. In 1950 a lower dining-hall was created in the basement of College so that the whole School could eat at once. The Call-over Hall had been used for whole-school announcements, but by 1946 this was too small and the School assembled in the open air in front of College. At the parade, the boys formed up in columns of three for announcements and the ceremony of awarding colours. The style of the occasion was military. Crichton-Miller's final move to accommodate his mushrooming school was to start a junior 'waiting' House. When a boarding house was full, new arrivals would be put here until there was room to take them. Number 96 Inverleith Place, just outside the School gates, was bought in 1951 and called Inverleith House, with Tony Timbs in charge. Number 98 was added when it came on the market two years later.

Where Ashcroft had been horror-stricken at the idea of public relations, Crichton-Miller took up with gusto the business of projecting his school and his own personality into the public consciousness. His success was a key factor in the rise in numbers. Crichton-Miller liked events which drew visitors into the School and in his first year started Masters' Guest Nights, and a ball on the eve of Founder's Day. On such occasions, the dignity and charm of his remarkable wife Monica were a precious asset. They had met at Cambridge and were to be married for 66 years. At Fettes her contribution in easing communication between the Lodge and masters and their wives was a key ingredient in the success of her husband's régime. He made a point of taking prospective parents round the School personally, and kept in close touch with prep schools. His taste for PR was not shared by all his staff. 'I found it profoundly distasteful,' wrote Graham Richardson, ' to be told to cultivate certain prep school masters, knowing that in entertaining them I had to sell a product.'

One effect of Crichton-Miller's efforts was to make the School better known in England. By 1951, 31 per cent of the boys had homes in England (52 per cent in Scotland), but by the end of the 1950s these positions were reversed, with 43.3

The new chancel, added to the Chapel in 1948, providing more room inside but disrupting Bryce's external roof line.

per cent coming from England. By advertising Fettes through the British Council, Crichton-Miller started to draw boys from a wider range of countries. South America had long been a source for pupils, but now a trickle of boys from Europe and Persia, Hong Kong and Canada appeared. They mainly went to Kimmerghame when it reopened. A strength of the School was that it drew from all classes, and if your parents were rich, you kept quiet about it. The rise in numbers meant a wider ethnic spread, but also a wider ability range, and some felt the atmosphere became less academic. The new Headmaster, however, was determined to cater properly for boys at every level of ability. In his first Founder's Day speech on 29th July 1946, he declared that Fettes had been renowned for her scholars, and he hoped that reputation would be sustained. 'But he also intended to give special attention to the mediocre people.' Though the phrase 'mediocre people' is one few modern headmasters would use, this had the ring of a decisive rejection of the academic élitism of former days as well as of the stranglehold of the Classics on the curriculum.

As the first non-classicist to be Headmaster, indeed, Crichton-Miller moved quickly to end the built-in dominance of the ancient languages. In his schooldays, he had himself been one of the despised 'Mods', and one of the few to win an Oxbridge award in a non-classical subject. Now in 1945, the classical Sixth was ejected from its time-honoured home in the 'Upper' where the horseshoe desk was carved with the initials of generations, and dispatched (significantly) to the Museum, where, as *The Fettesian* noted, it was watched over no longer by Juno and Apollo but by a bearded goat and a stuffed python. It was to end up later in a converted changing-room beside the west lavatories. The curriculum was completely re-cast and the old classical–modern distinction abolished in 1946. Everyone below the Sixth Form was now to study physics and chemistry, while the option choice for School Certificate was between Greek, history and applied maths. Each form was streamed into three. The Sixth Form was restructured, with more now sitting the Higher Certificate. By March 1946 *The Fettesian* could record: 'Drastic changes to the curriculum this term. All have to work for the Higher Certificate, being organised in Sixth Form groups according to the subjects they have chosen. No switching off after School Certificate.' But Crichton-Miller was careful to leave Oxbridge candidates in a special category. He was well aware of the PR value of Oxford and Cambridge Scholarships. Since science had been such a palpably second-class subject in the past, he moved fast to raise its profile by appointing talented teachers and upgrading facilities. The workshops, on the site of the North Building, were moved down to two huts which the Navy had put up during the War at Kimmerghame, and the old workshops transformed into laboratories. In 1947 biology was finally introduced into the Fettes curriculum. Crichton-Miller even applied some basic 'quality control' to school work. He issued an anonymous questionnaire to the boys to find out how much prep was being set and corrected in each subject. The answer was too little. He also took in a batch of exercise books each week, chosen at random, to monitor quality.

Unlike his predecessors, who taught the classical Sixth, Crichton-Miller aimed to teach the lower forms for one period a week for history or letter-writing. Although teaching was not his absolute *forte*, this habit, owed to Roxburgh's example at Stowe, meant he soon got to know a wide swathe of the boys, and it was important in helping him stay in close touch with the whole School, especially as its size increased. He was quite happy, indeed, to jump naked into the swimming pool among them, in the days before his successor introduced swimming trunks. The boys enjoyed the excitement generated by the new régime. *The Fettesian* editorial of December 1946 reported excitedly: 'Never in the history of Fettes has there been such a change as has been experienced this term.' As the main gate into Carrington Road and the main front door of College were opened, everyone picked up the feeling of a new beginning, and when the old board containing the School rules (signed by Dr Potts) which had survived for 76 years was removed early in 1947, a decisive break with the past was already signalled. The change in dress regulations in 1948 was not to everyone's taste, however. 'From the chrysalis of Top Hat and Tails erupted a prodigy called a "lumber jacket",' recorded Francis Pearson. This utility corduroy garment seemed 'perversely inappropriate', but was to survive as school dress for another 15 years. Discipline was put in the hands of an Adjutant. This demanding post was designed to test the mettle of up-and-coming young masters, and Tom Goldie-Scot and Charles Whittle in turn rose to the challenge.

The staff were predictably wary of the changes. Graham Richardson wrote: 'Many of Crichton-Miller's innovations were anathema to us: compulsory staff meetings after Chapel on Sundays; the marching of Houses up to breakfast after roll call in the morning.' Some masters were alienated by the patently low place they occupied in the esteem of the Headmaster. Crichton-Miller's order of priorities was: (1) Boys, (2) Parents, (3) Staff. He would put down colleagues (including his own Second Master) with little compunction. He is supposed to have said: 'I always reject ideas from the staff on principle. They get too big an idea of their importance otherwise.' He was a natural autocrat, known at Taunton as 'the Monarch', and at Fettes as 'the Pontiff'. It was said that two tactics (in order of preference) could be used to get an idea over to him: (1) make him think it was *his* idea, (2) put one of the boys up to suggesting it. His failure to listen to advice led to mistakes like the poor design of the extension to the North Building. He made the most sparing use of praise in dealing with members of staff. He always came, for instance, to plays, but instead of praising the director would usually ask why some particular hiccup had occurred. When George Preston had once toiled to make his play trouble-free, Crichton-Miller came up at the end merely to ask: 'Can we make sure next time that there are No Smoking notices in the auditorium?' Staff grudgingly respected his refusal to indulge in bland flattery, but longed for more encouragement. At the same time, Richardson admits, 'If he thought you were doing a good job, he left you to do it without interfering. He did indeed ask from you 20 per cent more than you felt capable of giving, and of course he got it. If he seldom praised, he rarely blamed.' As his grip on the School tightened, he felt no worries about going off each Tuesday to join the Linlithgow and Stirlingshire Hunt.

When in 1946 eight members of staff left (including some of the old guard), it

John Naiff teaching Physics in the 1950s. As the first non-classicist headmaster, Crichton-Miller made many reforms to end the dominance of ancient languages on the School curriculum, including the conversion of the old workshops into science laboratories, like this one, in the late 1940s. Note the corduroy lumber jackets.

The Staff Rugby Team in 1952. Front right is Crichton-Miller, sporting a Cambridge Blue sweater. Front centre is Peter Henderson, England cap and 1st XV coach.

G. C. Beamish, Housemaster of School House for 30 years until 1946.

was an early taste of his readiness to 'ease out' masters who didn't fit into his picture. In the case of J. V. Bayley-Brown (who had been off ill for a few months) he apparently did this by the simple expedient of announcing on Founder's Day 1948 that he was leaving. Nor did he make superhuman efforts to keep gifted performers like Bruce Mackenzie and 'Holy Bill' Aitken ('a man of enormous talent' wrote Ranald MacLean). Some went simply because they found his bulldozing methods unpalatable. As his school was in Edinburgh, he felt he could fill any vacancy with little trouble, but in spite of this, his Common Room was not the nursery of headmasters that Ashcroft's and, later, McIntosh's were. Three of Ashcroft's best appointments, Wilfred Hoare, Tom Goldie-Scot and Dick Cole-Hamilton, were among six pre-war masters who came back, among the 25 new arrivals in Crichton-Miller's first three years (only one a classicist, as John Blelloch noted). This injection of youthful talent rejuvenated the Common Room and generated *joie de vivre*, but turnover was to be far greater than in the past. It helped the economy of the School, since young masters were cheaper.

School House had been run single-handedly during the War by the avuncular G. C. Beamish, a slightly anti-establishment figure who had a special rapport with unathletic boys. When he left after 30 years of loyal service in 1946, Goldie-Scot and Cole-Hamilton were assigned to take over, and to divide it into two separate houses, College East and College West. Each first chose a Head of House, and a coin was then tossed to decide which of the two (Kemp Davidson and Henry Macintosh) would take first pick. They then went straight through a list of the 86 boys in College, choosing names for their House alternately. There were no married quarters in College, and the partnership of Dick and Tom was soon to be broken by their respective marriages, but their tradition was carried on by the talented quartet Dick Stoker, Duncan McCallum, George Booth and Peter Henderson. Foundationers (who paid no fees) were still all put in School House, and the intellectual distinction it derived from this combated any unsavoury prejudice which might surface towards them as 'free feeders', and helped to compensate for the fact that they had to live on four floors and kept changing their (bachelor) housemasters. In 1946, however, Crichton-Miller took the decision to distribute Foundationers round all the houses, reducing their number in the process. In Glencorse the problems of earlier days were being sorted out by Wilfred Hoare, followed by Tom Goldie-Scot when Hoare was appointed Headmaster of Strathallan, and Moredun was still under the stable regime of Freddy Macdonald. 'There was something about every boy from Moredun,' wrote Francis Pearson 'which reflected, however faintly, the splendid probity of the Housemaster.' Kimmerghame was taking time to settle down after a difficult recruitment process at the end of the War, but Graham Richardson and then from 1955 Dick Cole-Hamilton gave it the continuity and confidence it needed. Carrington was still run by its prefects. Tony Timbs, who went there in 1956, recalled that when he arrived: 'I found a formidable group of prefects headed by Gordon Waddell. They seemed to have taken complete control of the House. I was not on the agenda.'

Although the School's musical life had been kept going through the War by John Fairbairn, there was little else to occupy the boys' time beyond work and games until Crichton-Miller came. In his second year, he declared 6–7 p.m. each half-day 'activity hour', when everyone must either join in an activity or read silently in house. Too much spare time, he felt, spelt trouble, but, more importantly, it was crucial that every boy found something to excel at. Societies multiplied, and not only reels but model railways, debating, discussion groups (*Paramaecium*, *Cabal* and *Hyperon*), drama and bell-ringing flourished. Fettes drama had been patchy up till now, and the highlights had been inspired by individuals like John Hay Beith, whose play *The Crimson Cocoanut* had been premiered at Fettes in 1908, and Ian Harvey who, as a boy, had combined with Henry Havergal to write operettas like *Prometheus Unwound* in 1933. In 1940 Dick Cole-Hamilton had produced the first house play. Now, from 1948, Fettes drama took off. The leading figures were George Booth and musician Tommy Evans, who ambitiously staged *The Bartered Bride* in 1948, and in 1950 *Der Freischutz* (the first production in Britain since 1890). Booth was an unconventional and provocative cleric with a flair for the stage, who produced from 1949 a series of serious classic plays ranging from Ibsen, Chekhov and Shaw through Fry to T. S. Eliot. Many boys found such productions heavy going (especially *Murder in the Cathedral*), but the quality was plain to see, and helped to get across to outsiders who swelled the audience a perception of excellence pervading everything the School was doing.

This excellence was also seen on the games field. Encouraged by Ian Sutcliffe, PE specialist, who burst on to the scene in his Allard open tourer in 1947, a wide range of sports flourished. Ian's effervescence and good nature compelled enthusiasm

H. F. Macdonald, the remarkably successful Housemaster of Moredun and later Second Master: painting by Sir William Hutchison.

Reg Hollingdale (with bat) and Charles Whittle (in blazer) coaching Richard Bowman and Donald Steel in the School nets.

for things physical. Fives, squash, tennis, shooting, boxing, swimming, basketball, fencing and athletics all prospered, and by 1949 there were matches in nine different sports. Everyone did two sessions a week of physical education, and facilities for tennis, basketball, swimming, and gym were steadily upgraded. Athletics was given a lift by the construction of a new track. The site (to the north of the Below field) was on a slope, so Crichton-Miller simply hired a bulldozer and did the job with Ian Sutcliffe and a team of boys. Each had to give up six hours of his time a term. When the ground was duly flattened, a surface of cinder was laid down, and by the summer of 1954 the Sports was held on it for the first time. Because the track was long and thin, the bends were very tight, but it did service for 40 years. Performances meanwhile improved dramatically as athletes like Iain Bain with his hammer and James Wellwood with his pole reached standards unmatched at any school. The 1st XI cricket (coached by Charles Whittle and professional Reg Hollingdale and strengthened by players of the calibre of Graham Cumming and Donald Steel) reached new heights, and the first three XIs were undefeated in 1953 and 1954.

All this variety on the games menu did not, however, detract from the School's premier game. The School's name was still synonymous with rugby success, and in the 30 years to 1949, more Fettesians had won Oxford or Cambridge Blues than the products of any other school in the land. Now during the 1950s, helped by the surge in school numbers, rugby standards reached an extraordinary height. Peter Henderson, historian and England rugby cap, had been appointed in 1948, to be joined as 1st XV coach in 1952 by Bruce McKenzie. Under their guidance, and with a steady flow of gifted players providing the fire-power for a run of superlative XVs, the School team was unbeaten in Scotland between 1950 and late 1956. By

Rossall Rugby match, 1954, during the 1st XV's remarkable run of success when it was unbeaten for 6 years.

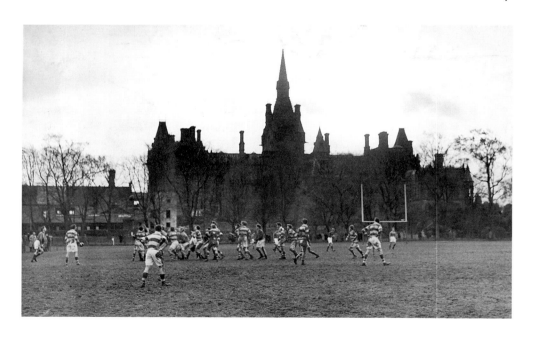

1955, not a boy in the School had seen the 1st XV beaten in a school match. It was an unparalleled run of success. When on 20th October 1956 the captain of Merchiston drop-kicked a late penalty from the touch-line which bounced on the bar and crept over to give them victory by 6 - 5, there was a mixture of disappointment and relief. The strain of the assumption of invincibility had become a cross for the players to bear. 'Inevitably,' wrote Francis Pearson, 'the longer the winning sequence, the more desperately the line was guarded; an undue weight came to be attached to defence; and there were those who, however proud, secretly desired a healthy defeat.' In 1953, the pairing of David Horne and Gordon Waddell was so effective that a correspondent in *The Scotsman* suggested that the Scottish XV would do better if they could import the Fettes halves. The rugby strength was in depth, and in 1954 the first four XVs won all their school matches, scoring 602 points against 50. Blues and international caps were harder to win by the 1940s, but this did not stop Old Fettesians complaining at the shortage of Fettesian Blues. One, writing to *The Fettesian* in July 1947, felt moved to explain this by the intrusion of soccer into the School. 'Our famous rugby Blues,' he wrote, 'would be shocked to see some of our senior rugby men playing soccer on a summer's evening.' Not so, riposted the Editor, recalling the account in the first edition of *The Fettesian* of the 1st XV of 1877 (which produced four Blues and two international caps): 'In addition to our rugby matches we also played two under Association rules . . . it greatly improves dribbling.'

Gym class with Ian Sutcliffe, the dynamic P. E. specialist appointed in 1946.

Alongside games, academic standards held up, and Oxbridge scholarships were still won in Classics, but also now in history, English, maths and science. The year 1953 stood out, with seven academic awards won. In spite of his efforts to stop Classics monopolizing the curriculum, Crichton-Miller was still the first to appreciate the successes the subject derived from the teaching of Freddy Macdonald and a series of clever Sixth Form tutors. On Founder's Day 1955, as if to stress that *plus ça change, plus c'est la même chose*, he said: 'It is my considered opinion that, by and large, the best training we give here is still in Classics among the academic subjects, and in rugby football among the games.' There was, however, no distinctive intellectual culture to complement the prevailing rugby culture, and Crichton-Miller's selection of prefects was apt to promote the values of athleticism. In this *milieu*, non-games players could suffer, but the rugby culture was a unifying force in the School and a focus for passionate loyalty.

One or two events stand out in the onward march of the 1950s. In the early hours of Saturday 29th March 1952, fire broke out on the top floor of Carrington. Ludovic Stuart, coming back to the House after midnight from an illegal visit 'up town', was the first to realise it was on fire. He ran up the fire escape and, pausing only to undress and put on his pyjamas to avert suspicion, raised the alarm. The next morning Sandy Lindsay, Clerk of Works, and his team tackled the mopping-up operation, fretting that they would miss the Cup Final that afternoon, but when midday came they found themselves dispatched in the School van with a packed lunch to Glasgow for the game by the Headmaster, who joined in the afternoon's clear-up himself. The burnt-out dormitory was reconstructed to provide room for

A cartoon of Crichton-Miller on the touch line.

The morning after the blaze in Carrington, 29th March 1952: photograph from The Scotsman.

The Drill Squad at the Tattoo on Founder's Day, 1954, which was never repeated in the same form.

three more boys, and was ready for rehabitation by the Autumn Term.

In 1954 Crichton-Miller planned a Tattoo to bring Founder's Day to an end. The impact of the reels was impaired when Pipe Instructor McGregor fell making his way through the bushes to his hidden post, knocking all his drones out of tune, so that the reels were accompanied throughout by an unearthly wailing noise. The Tattoo was never repeated in the same form, but the Retreat was retained as a regular feature of Founder's Day, with its haunting close late at night, as, after the flags were lowered and the 'Last Post' sounded by a bugler from the roof of College, the Band marched away across the Below Fields in the last rays of the setting sun, their playing fading gradually into the distance. There was a real loss in atmosphere when the Retreat had to be moved to tea-time to meet parental needs.

The visit of the Queen and the Duke of Edinburgh in 1955 was a suitable climax to a decade of remarkable change. Two hundred and twenty-five boys were on display in activities like cricket, piping and reels in a show of 'organised spontaneity'. Everything went smoothly, and, as a sequel to the visit, the gravel area immediately to the east of College was cleared and a new lawn to be called 'The Queen's Grass' was laid by a hundred boys on Field day. As he showed the Queen round his school, Crichton-Miller could look back with satisfaction on the results of the first ten years of his headship. The buildings he showed off to her were a solid witness to his energy. The last phase, after the new gym was built, had involved converting the old gym into a concert-hall in 1953 (removing the cupola and its supporting pillars) and building a new block for music and art. The Sanatorium had been reorganised, leaving Malcolm House to provide rooms for bachelor masters, a change noted in the 1952 'Vive-La':

Malcolm House, which once reeked of specifics and plasters,
Now reeks of the vices of bachelor masters.

On Founder's Day that year, Crichton-Miller announced that the ten-year building plan had cost over £100,000, 'but very little from the pockets of parents.' Private and public sources had been tapped, and the Old Fettesians, with whom he had been on excellent terms, had responded warmly. All this had been supervised by his loyal lieutenant, Sandy Lindsay, the Clerk of Works, and 'generations who use this place in the future will enjoy the fruits of his devoted labour.'

John Rae, who did his teaching practice at Fettes in the same year, records his impressions of the Donald Crichton-Miller of 1955. 'It was my first encounter with a charismatic leader. Crichton-Miller was treated by the staff and by his pupils as though he possessed superhuman powers . . . His reputation as the strong man of the public school world made him something of a talisman for the pupils of other schools as well. When he arrived on the touchline at the start of an inter-school rugby match, the rival groups of spectators cheered and counter-cheered as though he was the president of the games and the visiting Headmaster counted for nothing.' Crichton-Miller could still be high-handed with his staff, as when in 1956 a group of school prefects was found ensconced in the janitor's room smoking. When they defended themselves by saying that this had been going on for years with the

Harold Bond, the Bursar 1947–76, who was one of Crichton-Miller's first recruits to the School staff; George Cooper, the Steward, 1936–61; Alex 'Sandy' Lindsay, the Clerk of Works, 1925–62, in 1953.

The visit of the Queen (escorted by Crichton-Miller) and the Duke of Edinburgh, 1955.

The staff photograph, 1958.

connivance of masters, Crichton-Miller summoned staff and prefects together for a meeting at which he openly invited prefects to incriminate individual masters, before expelling the school prefects concerned and sacking the janitor. It caused deep resentment, as well as amazement at what seemed an extraordinary over-reaction. His system had always been based on a close partnership between himself and his prefects, and he felt strangely let down. Staff wives, however, found him charming, and he extended to them (especially the younger ones) a gallantry and thoughtfulness their spouses did not always receive.

His self-confidence pervaded his public utterances. He was a fine speaker, and

James Bond's entry in Who's Who, *according to Ian Fleming.*

BOND, Commander James, C.M.G. 1954; Principal Officer, Civil Service since 1953; *b.* 1924; *s.* of Andrew Bond of Glencoe, (*d.* 1935), and Monique (nee Delacroix). of Canton de Vaud, (*d.* 1935); *m.* 1962, Teresa (*d.* 1962), *o.d.* Marc-Ange Draco, Marseilles; no *c.* Educ.: Eton College and Fettes. Joined what is now Ministry of Defence, 1941; drafted Special Branch, R.N.V.R. Ended war service 1946, Commander; rejoined Ministry of Defence. *Recreations:* Golf, gambling, motoring and underwater swimming. *Address:* c/o Ministry of Defence.

Ranald MacLean noted that, even when guest speakers on Founder's Day were as formidable as Robert Bruce-Lockhart in 1953, Selwyn Lloyd (Minister of Defence) in 1955, and Iain Macleod (Minister of Labour) in 1957, he was not outshone. Lloyd and Macleod, now rising fast in the Government, were helping to confirm the perception of Fettes as a nursery of politicians, while Bruce-Lockhart (whose extraordinary life included a spell in prison in the Kremlin in 1918 for allegedly plotting to assassinate Lenin) was one of those claimed to have been the original of Ian Fleming's James Bond, who is stated by Fleming in *You Only Live Twice* to have been a Fettesian. Bond, wrote Fleming, started at Eton, but after 'some alleged trouble with one of the boys' maids,' his aunt 'managed to obtain his transfer to Fettes, his father's old school. Here the atmosphere was somewhat Calvinistic, and both academic and athletic standards were rigorous.'

Donald Crichton-Miller, 1958.

Life at Fettes in the 1950s was no longer exactly Calvinistic, but it was still rigorous. 'The Fettes of my time,' wrote Francis Pearson, 'took itself very seriously. Whether a more light-hearted approach was compatible with the strenuous ethic of the School is at least a matter of doubt.' There are maybe too many storm-clouds in the youthful sky. 'Does any schoolboy enjoy more than fugitive moments of happiness?' he asks. The answer might be 'yes' if the schoolboy was a School Prefect or in the 1st XV, content to enjoy the adulation of his peers – until he left, that is, since never again would he find himself such a focus for admiration.

The same was true of the Headmaster. He had begun to feel he had done his job, and that it was time to give way to someone who would stress the academic side, since at the end of the day he was not much interested in what was being taught in all his classrooms. When in 1958 the Governors of Stowe invited Crichton-Miller to leave Fettes and take over their school 'as a hatchet man to get rid of the dead wood on the staff' in John Rae's words, it was the end of 13 years of creative upheaval. The astonishment was to come when five years later he was forced to resign the job he had gone to. Methods more drastic than those he had employed at Fettes were a bitter pill that Stowe could not swallow. Rae found it 'inconceivable that so powerful a Headmaster could be persuaded to resign.' Meeting Bob Roberts soon after the debacle, Crichton-Miller roared at him '"No good, old boy. I've had to go. It was either them or me", as if he'd just come in from a day's hunting.' His achievement at Fettes, however, remained a lasting monument to his leadership. He had dominated the community with his presence. He had more than doubled the numbers, from 211 to 459, given the School immense self-belief, new facilities and a sound economy and, to a remarkable extent, had come to personify the School. He was, with little doubt, the man for his time.

79

6

Keeping the Lid On
McINTOSH : 1958–71

It has been for centuries the pride of the Scottish educational system that it allows talent to rise. The 'lad o'pairts' (Scots for 'gifted boy') could win through from any home background. In the case of Ian McIntosh, the first home-grown Scot to be Headmaster of Fettes, his schooling did not take off until he arrived at Inverness Academy at the age of 14. The son of a peripatetic piano-tuner, he had moved through a succession of schools and often had to miss classes because of asthma attacks. In Inverness, however, he found his feet and met his future wife, Florence. He went on to Aberdeen University, gaining a First in modern languages and winning a Scholarship to Trinity, Cambridge, where he won another First and a soccer Blue. His ability had made its mark by unflinching effort, and the identification of hard work with success was something that never left him. His career was to be driven by the Presbyterian work ethic.

He taught first at Bradfield, and at Winchester, where he stayed for 16 years, became Head of Languages and fell in love with the English Public School system. He responded to the Wykehamist ideals of concern for the individual and the pursuit of excellence for its own sake, and the influence of the School remained with him ever afterwards. In 1953 he was appointed Headmaster of George Watson's in Edinburgh (where he had applied ten years earlier but was thought too young at 35). At Watson's his administrative skill and brilliance as a teacher were recognised. *The Watsonian* of May 1958 described his teaching technique as 'superbly presented in the grand manner': 'His Sixth Form pupils relished the impressive entrance, the pacing up and down behind the long lecture room desk, the rapidly-spoken, highly-charged sentences aimed at the back of the ceiling, followed by a pause and a slow, reflective "Yes", as though the thoughts just expressed were being reconsidered and found acceptable.' When Donald Crichton-Miller left Fettes, McIntosh found the temptation to re-enter the boarding *milieu* he had so loved at Winchester too strong to resist, though he had spent only five years at Watson's. Crichton-Miller pressed for his appointment, and in September of 1958 he became Headmaster of Fettes. There was dismay at Watson's. This was a great school, and its Headmasters simply did *not* stay as short a time as five years. It did not help that he was going to an upmarket local rival.

Facing page: *the School Tower floodlit for the Centenary;* below: *Ian McIntosh on his arrival at Fettes.*

Cardinal Heard and 'Caesar', the School Porter in 1960.

McIntosh brought great virtues to his new post, but an ironic twist of fate had assigned to the reign of this natural conservative the most turbulent period of social change in the history of the School. At interview the Governors had stressed to him the need to lift the School's academic standards, since they felt the recent surge in numbers had pulled in boys with low Common Entrance marks who gave a philistine flavour to the community. McIntosh's instinct was to agree that a school is for producing scholars, but, at the same time, he was anxious not to sabotage the School's formidable reputation for rugby in the process. He was all too conscious that his own Blue was a soccer one, and the tag 'wrong shape of ball' had gone before him. 'What consternation his appointment must have caused,' said Eric James in ironic mood years later, 'to some Old Fettesians who had hoped for a recruit from some really great rugby club like St. Helen's or Wigan!' McIntosh carefully suppressed his own enthusiasm for the round ball. When on one occasion two Fettesians including Henry Gibson, an avid Hibs fan, had slipped away without permission from a Saturday 1st XV match to Easter Road for the Hearts match, they were horrified to see their Headmaster standing with his son two rows behind them on the terraces. 'I think we'd *all* better keep quiet about this!' said McIntosh.

He worked hard to play the part of a rugby enthusiast, but early results let him down. George Watson's, who had never beaten Fettes in his five years there, proceeded to win every game during his first five years at Fettes. The word went round the old boys that the new Headmaster was failing to preserve the School's precious rugby reputation. But there is no evidence that McIntosh, who was passionately keen on cricket, took concrete steps to moderate the cult of athleticism. Indeed, in a remarkable speech one Commem, he declared that no schoolboy game was worth playing unless it had an element of physical danger in it. The rugby fraternity found him extremely supportive, and he signed up gifted coaches like John Herbert and Ian Robertson (later to coach Cambridge to a remarkable run of success in the Varsity match).

The truth was that the School had by now few of the gifted players who had given such distinction to the rugby teams of the early 1950s, and that there was growing competition from other schools. When there were fewer victories for the boys to admire, they started to ask the awkward questions, to complain that too much rugby was being played by the unathletic, to point out its deficiencies as a way of spending the afternoons. It was, after all, compulsory, and in the 1960s compulsion was to become anathema. School activities were meanwhile increasingly reaching out to the world outside the School gates, and the 'Outside Service', started by the chaplain George Buchanan-Smith and Ronald Guild (who ran the CCF but believed passionately in community education), involved getting out to help the old and disabled, and opened the eyes of the boys to the very different society of, for example, the housing estates that had mushroomed in the space between the northern periphery of the grounds and the Firth of Forth.

The school routine was broken in 1960 by an Inspection (which reported warmly on the School's performance) and by the visit of Cardinal Heard. The fact that a Fettesian who was also the son of a former Headmaster was ascending the promotion ladder in the Roman Church seemed curiously improbable, but no Calvinist scruples stopped McIntosh making a good thing of it. There was one snag. Local Protestants used the west gate pillar for chalking up the message 'Kick the Pope', and the Cardinal was due to pass that way. A party was sent out the night before to rub out the graffito, but by the time Heard arrived in the morning it was back again, and the Cardinal's chaplain had to hold up his wide-brimmed hat to make sure it hid the offending text. The 'Vive-La' that year foresaw further promotion for the Cardinal:

Those who chalk on our gates must now cherish the hope
That one day they may kick a Fettesian Pope.

As the School advanced into the 1960s, however, Ian McIntosh became ill at ease. The strain of headmastering began to tell, and even in the holidays it took time to unwind. He was always working, and even at home in front of the television he would have a board on his lap for writing. The natural loneliness of a Headmaster's job was compounded by insecurity and an acute sense of propriety which distanced him from boys and staff and could make him seem pompous and authoritarian. He could see the effects of inhibition clearly enough in others. Of one straitlaced pupil, he said to David Pighills: 'With that sort of boy, I feel like saying: "Here's £2. Go out and get drunk."' His own inhibitions were harder to deal with. On his study desk there was a notice saying 'Don't just sit there, worry!' and

Clearing up after another fire in Carrington, February 1963.

83

A cartoon of Ronnie Selby-Wright, a regular visitor to the School chapel services, drawn by Tom Curr.

George Buchanan-Smith, School Chaplain and Housemaster of Glencorse, 'a formidable School character'.

he was too prone to take its advice. When he did manage to relax, another self came through – charming, witty, a scintillating conversationalist. The poems he wrote for occasional gatherings were famously clever, and it was a delightful moment at the end of a good dinner party when he sat at the piano and played Scott Joplin. Staff in trouble found his advice incisive and warmly sympathetic – especially in a crisis, like the one that struck Patrick Croker in March 1963 when a freak accident on the way back from Arduous Training Camp caused the death of a gifted and delightful boy, James Heatley. His Headmaster's advice and sympathy were long remembered and helped Patrick over the trauma, but McIntosh himself was deeply upset by the tragedy. He almost gave up. Was the job worth the candle when this could happen to one of his boys? That Easter the pressure was almost unbearable, and only a holiday on the Loire with his old friend from Winchester days, James Mansel, restored his spirits and energy. Meanwhile, the rebuilding of the Carrington studies was pressing, since the House had had another fire at the end of February. The boys had been rash enough to put on a play called *Out of the Frying Pan*, and a week later the study area went up. The headline in the *Evening News* ran 'Fettes boys Flee Fire', but in fact the House had been evacuated safely and in good order.

By 1963, however, Ian McIntosh could chalk up plenty of things on the credit side. He had made a series of first-rate appointments, creating a strong Common Room. 'It is my conviction,' said David McMurray, 'that the Common Room when I joined it in 1964 was the most convivial, happiest, friendliest and most united group of teachers working in any school in the country.' The appointments injected excitement into the School's academic life, and the School was quick to take up 'Nuffield Biology' and construct a language laboratory, presided over by Kenneth Collier, as well as being the first in Scotland, under Sydney Brewer's guidance, to pilot the Schools Mathematics Project. Oxbridge awards were still being won in an ever more competitive market, especially still in the Classics, though history was taught by Patrick Croker 'with a verve and enthusiasm that must be truly exceptional,' thought Arthur Sanderson. The English Department was outstanding and Science was moving ahead under John Naiff. The drama tradition was being finely sustained by Bob Roberts and Edward Gage, with even house plays (like Gage's *The Lark* or Michael Lester-Cribb's *Le bourgeois Gentilhomme*) showing distinction, and Gage was energizing the Art Department.

Chapel services were livened up by the innovations of Chaplains George Buchanan-Smith and Richard Gorrie, by Michael Lester-Cribb's fireworks at the organ and by inspirational visits from Ronnie Selby-Wright. The days when Potts had refused to appoint a chaplain were past, and after the War men like Stephen Floyd, George Booth and Bill Aitken had looked after the School's spiritual needs. Buchanan-Smith, who had previously worked in the slums of New York and Glasgow, was soon a formidable school character, with his catch-phrases like 'Don't blame the Church!' Like Aitken, he was not the man to shield privileged schoolboys from the real world. Down to earth and principled, he became the conscience of the School, and often enough boys and masters alike shifted uneasily in their pews as his sermons hit a raw nerve. Their message of mutual understanding was

not lost. Bit by bit the atmosphere in the School was becoming gentler, more tolerant, more open to the outside world. 'We still had fagging and beating,' recalled David Agassiz, 'but there was a greater caring and sensitivity than folklore attributed to the past.'

The face of the Fettes estate was changing, as acquisitive eyes were cast at such a large green area within the expanding city. For some time 18 acres at the northwest corner of the grounds had been earmarked in the City Development Plan for an eventual Technical College. By 1963 the site was claimed for the Telford College, and around the same time 14 acres between Carrington and Comely Bank were sold to the Corporation for £38,700 for the new Police Headquarters and playing fields. The Governors had agreed to this deal under pressure, knowing that they always had 15 acres in reserve for possible future growth to the east of the police plot (then leased to the University for playing fields), but in the same year the City of Edinburgh issued a compulsory purchase Order for this piece of ground for a new mixed Secondary School to replace the old Broughton School. It was the last

An aerial view of the School estate. Notice the newly built Broughton Secondary School (above the College building) and the Police Headquarters on the right of the picture.

85

Pupils from Fettes and Broughton School chat together after a rehearsal for a combined concert. Harmony between the two schools has lately been improving.

Below: *the new dining hall opened in 1966; below right: Arniston, the new boarding house, opened in 1967.*

straw for the School, which vigorously contested the Order, but at a Public Enquiry in the City Chambers in April 1965 its appeal was turned down. The Enquiry concluded that the School had enough playing field space elsewhere, with a tenth of an acre per boy, 'as much as a Public School can expect to have these days when it has the misfortune to be situated within the confines of a large city,' as well as the luxury of its own golf course. The Order would go through, but this would mark an end to the appropriation of the School's land. Some felt the Governors should have pre-empted the Order by establishing an active use of the site, and were also worried about the potential for friction with an independent and maintained school confronting each other across Carrington Road. Broughton School itself was not built until 1972, and worst fears have not been fulfilled. Apart from periodic flare-ups (notably after falls of snow when the snowball proved an irresistible weapon in the class war), there has been an uneasy peace and latterly some sign of a growth in mutual respect. The only gain for the School in the sales was that they provided a spring-board for the major building programme that followed. The School's Centenary was coming up in 1970, and in 1964 Ian McIntosh officially launched the Centenary Development Campaign and Appeal, with the aim of building a new dining hall and boarding house, and creating a new library. When a science school was later added to these, it made up the most ambitious new building programme since the start of the School.

The path to the Centenary in 1970, however, was destined to be a rocky one. First of all, rumblings of political action against the independent schools were growing more insistent. The Wilson Government of 1964 came into power with a manifesto commitment to integrate them into the state system. The Newsom Commission was set up amidst great trepidation, but its Report in 1968 turned out to be a damp squib.

The threat to the stability of traditional public school structures from changing social mores was much more menacing. As the advance of the permissive society

moved into top gear in the middle of the 'swinging sixties', everything came into question. A movement created by adults to suit themselves was soon taken over by the younger generation, and when the satire of the media found its *raison d'être* in the ridicule of all established authority, the habit was infectious. In 1965, Ian McIntosh preached a sermon on the difference between satire and cynicism. The satire of Gilray and Swift, he argued, was positive, pointing towards reform, while the cynicism of *Private Eye* or the cult programme *That Was the Week that Was* sought first to sneer, then destroy. He did not like the way things were shaping. Unrest in the universities soon filtered into schools, and discontent was building up when in 1968 the film *If* came out, backed by American money and depicting an archaic school where the boys finally run riot and gun down the teachers. At the same time the pop culture was giving solidarity to the younger generation and shutting out adults.

The whole movement appalled McIntosh. His predecessors had been able to rely on the 'unchanging verities', the pillars of public school life he had come to admire at Winchester. What could come next if they were to crumble? 'Routine, status, hierarchy,' wrote John Rae, 'provided security and an anaesthetic against the pain of self-questioning.' Now all authority was challenged, all compulsions queried. A few boys professed an egalitarian motive, most just wanted more chance to enjoy themselves, to go out, smoke, drink, meet girls. McIntosh thought such hedonistic impulses dangerous. He had told housemasters, for example, never to offer wine to their prefects. Hair became the *casus belli*, since long hair was the badge of the pop culture, just as short hair spelt compulsion and adulthood. But if long hair was to be banned, who was to say at what point hair becomes long? The boys were quick to exploit this dilemma. Eric Anderson, Housemaster of Arniston and an expert on Sir Walter Scott, kept a bust of Scott in his hall. If your hair was longer than Sir Walter's, it was too long – a fair deal, since the great novelist was not a short-back-and-sides man. McIntosh, however, became thoroughly irritated with the non-conformers. He bumped into one of them near the barber's shop one day, Tony Blair, the future Prime Minister, and seized his chance. He took him straight in and stood there, unrelenting as the cherished mop was trimmed.

Boys' boarding schools bore the worst brunt of the revolution, but in Scotland its force was slightly cushioned. South of the Border, as the artillery was trained on the sacred cows of the system, many headmasters gave way on the old compulsions, though most did it grudgingly and selectively. McIntosh, with his strong Christian faith, was not addicted to compromise. His instinct was to batten down the hatches and ride out the storm. He saw something actively immoral in the concept of a permissive society, and where values were at stake it was weakness to cave in, however unpopular it might make you.

By 1968 'there was a feeling of pent-up frustration throughout the School,' wrote Patrick Anketell-Jones. Compulsion of most sorts was resented. In order to create some sort of dialogue, McIntosh called together the following year's prefects for a discussion. Few were as content with existing structures as Carrington, which under Michael Leslie remained a bastion of traditional practice. *The Carrington New*

Man's Guide of 1968 still reminded the new arrival that 'all Fettesians are referred to as "men", not "boys", and woe betide any man who uses the word "boy",' that prefects are called 'Sir', that 'it is to the Head of House that all complaints must be rendered, and if he thinks fit he may refer the matter to the Housemaster,' and that 'it is not a regular habit for men to associate frequently with other men more than a year junior or senior to them.' The prefects raised with McIntosh the issues of more leave out, compulsory rugby, and the problem of making people stick to minute dress regulations like 'middle button of jacket to be buttoned up at all times.' At the meeting, he accepted that 'piddling' regulations should be dropped, but that more revolutionary suggestions needed longer consideration. This in essence meant little change, and the meeting had few concrete results. He was by now not a consensus man, and when Head of School Sandy Pratt came to ask for a new concession, his answer was a self-mocking one: 'I'd like to hear everything you have to say before I say "no".' To the boys, clothes were heavily symbolic, and to join the club you needed the top button of your shirt undone, your tie at half-mast and some sort of coloured T-shirt visible in the gap. Wearing unpolished zipper boots, you either strummed your own guitar or listened to Leonard Cohen, Led Zeppelin, the Doors or the Beatles. You did not, however, use drugs. In *A Hundred Years of Fettes* McIntosh wrote that he was for 'progressive liberalisation where it seemed appropriate.' In practice he was always worried that change would undermine some essential principle. This seems to have stopped him ending things like personal fagging which

The calm before the storm: McIntosh relaxes with his short-haired, well-turned-out prefects in 1963, confident in their domination of the School.

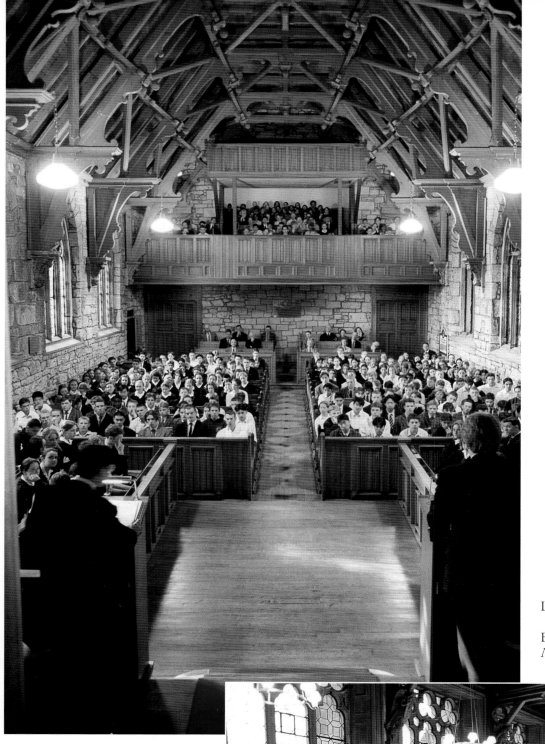

Left: *a service in the Chapel.*

Below: *a recent picture of the New Library, opened in 1970.*

Charles Whittle, Housemaster of Moredun, holds forth, over-looked by a stag's head.

by now were not the real world. Michael Lester-Cribb and Eric Anderson had already done away with it in their houses, but prefects elsewhere were loth to let it go. McIntosh valued it as providing 'the experience of doing things for other people,' but he was ahead of many schools in ending beating of boys by boys. In spite of everything, though, Fettes avoided the hints of outright revolt that surfaced in other schools, like petitions, demonstrations in Chapel and worse.

As McIntosh kept his finger in the dyke, 'at times,' said Dick Cole-Hamilton, 'he must have felt terribly alone, like Horatius, holding the bridge against the barbarians.' In fact, though, he was not alone, and the solidarity and quality of the staff saw him through. 'We were all devoted to him,' said David McMurray. 'We all respected 100 per cent his integrity.' While they complained that he was inflexible, they admired his principles. Though the indomitable Freddy Macdonald had retired in 1962, Tom Goldie-Scot and Dick Cole-Hamilton helped to give the authority structure weight and humanity. Many of the housemasters of the 1960s and early 1970s were of a quite remarkable calibre. Charles Whittle, appointed to Moredun by Crichton-Miller, was in his idiosyncratic way a tower of strength, and in his hour of need McIntosh could be glad of the powerful appointments he had made, including the future headmasters of Strathallan, Loretto and Oundle, Stamford, Abingdon, Shrewsbury and Eton, Bishop's Stortford, Alleyn's, St Alban's G.S., Wrekin and Gresham's, Holt.

Ian Sutcliffe, the games master, was the presiding genius of the Common Room, which in the 1960s was a happy place. The warmth of his personality dissi-

Facing page: *The main building from the front, 1992.*

pated friction and welded the staff into a unit. As a coach, he was as interested in the inept squash player as the rugby star, and he organised the complicated games programme by making notes on the back of a succession of cigarette packets. Few staff were staying long enough to develop the eccentricities of an earlier generation, but some of the non-teaching staff showed real loyalty and staying power, like Jimmy Skeldon, Harry Headspeath, George Douglas, Sarah McManus, Theresa Lavelle, Reg Hollingdale and Nurse Fenton. Nurse Fenton (known as Battleaxe) stood like Cerberus at the portals of the Sanatorium, where patients who survived their first encounter discovered a heart of gold. The loyalty of the staff is borne out by the fact that there were only five Stewards and four heads of Maintenance in the School's history up to 1998, when George Stenhouse retired. Between 1885 and 1975 there were only three cricket professionals, and, between 1872 and 1952, only three matrons at the Sanatorium.

As the 1960s moved on, the School was building up towards the Centenary. The Appeal had had a splendid response, and the new dining hall opened in 1966. This strikingly designed building had over-run its budget, but in use it was an instant success, presided over by Fred Broughton. The new boarding house, Arniston, was meanwhile being completed to the east of the Below Fields. It came into emergency use earlier than expected when in June 1967 a fire broke out in Glencorse. The Glencorse boys moved into the Sanatorium and Arniston (sleeping on the floor) as George Buchanan-Smith took over. As the opening of Arniston approached, the bachelor masters moved into Inverleith Place from Malcolm House, which joined the Sanatorium in becoming the temporary Glencorse.

McIntosh and his wife, Florence, performing the Centenary tree planting by the West Drive.

90

The Queen Mother's visit, part of the Centenary celebrations. She meets (above left) *staff and pupils*, and (above, from left) *Jimmy Skeldon, Reg Hollingdale and Harry Headspeath, representing between them more than 100 years of service to Fettes.*

Sir William Fettes dictates his will in The Fettes Masque: David McMurray in full flow.

Arniston (intended to relieve pressure in the other houses) opened under Eric Anderson in September 1967. He recruited the House throughout the age range with volunteers, though Kimmerghame (whose members were fiercely loyal to Dick Cole-Hamilton) provided only two volunteers, one of them Tony Blair. The 'house visitor' was Knox Cunningham, an Irish MP who delighted in stirring up boys like Blair with inflammatory pronouncements and encouraging them to question everything. Meanwhile, the old dining hall was turned into a handsome library, and in 1969 the Science School was begun. As the Western General Hospital expanded up to the rear of Moredun Crescent (the terrace of staff houses beyond the west gate), a deal was struck with the hospital by Richard Winnington-Ingram, the assistant bursar. Moredun Crescent was demolished and six new staff houses ('West Woods') built for staff inside the grounds at the west end of the playing fields.

The Centenary in 1970 was the climax of McIntosh's time. The opening of the Science School by the Queen Mother in September completed an unprecedented building programme. Although McIntosh had shrunk from a full updating of the boarding houses, regarding study bedrooms as 'dens of iniquity', the new dining hall, Science School and Arniston House were a glittering witness to the success of the Centenary Appeal. The Centenary events themselves were superbly organised – the Ball in the Assembly Rooms, *The Fettes Masque*, the floodlighting of the School, Founder's Day and Commemoration. Four publications, *A Hundred Years of Fettes*, *The Fettes Register*, *The Centenary Supplement* and *Our Founder Sir William Fettes* marked the occasion. On Founder's Day, McIntosh gave a characteristically brilliant and witty speech, and Eric James, Vice-Chancellor of York University, responded in kind, picking up the burning topic of authority: 'There is an overriding authority greater than any of us – and don't let's forget that even the youngest of us may be wrong. It is the authority of truth . . . We ought to be sceptical,' but with 'the scepticism of Socrates, not of David Frost.' At *The Fettes Masque*, a wonderful kaleidoscope of the first 100 years put together by Tim Butchard, audiences could share the School's pride.

Centenary year also saw Selwyn Lloyd's appointment as Speaker of the House of Commons and the death of Iain Macleod. Some had tipped Macleod, the finest debater of his day in the House, to become the first Fettesian Prime Minister, but when Tory grandee Lord Salisbury called him 'too clever by half', it did not help his cause. Michael Foot earlier said he had the 'disadvantage of not having been at Eton': 'I think that he went to some glorified, poshed-up secondary school in Scotland' ('"poshed-up", my foot' noted Freddy Macdonald in *The Fettesian*).

Meanwhile, McIntosh had made an extraordinary concession. He had admitted a girl. For almost 100 years the School had been a girl-free zone. By 1965 Michael Lester-Cribb had started joint concerts with St. George's, but there were few opportunities for social mixing apart from occasional house dances. These were grisly occasions. A consignment of girls was ordered in advance from a school like Cranley or St Denis' by the apprehensive housemaster, and as soon as they arrived, each boy's aim was to pounce on a presentable girl and hang on to her for the evening. The housemaster and his tutors, feeling painfully *de trop*, prowled round looking for couples who got too close (or, worse, horizontal), while the boys wished the adults would drop through the floorboards. Then in 1968 advertising supremo David Ogilvy came to deliver the speech at Founder's Day. He quoted the Founder's will, with its reference to 'young people'. 'What right had the first Governors,' he declaimed, 'to decide that our Founder meant only *boy* children? He clearly intended that this great school should educate girls as well as boys. If the Governors continue to ignore his wishes, I urge you boys to follow the example of

The Fettes Masque: *'Have you never loved in Latin, boy?'*

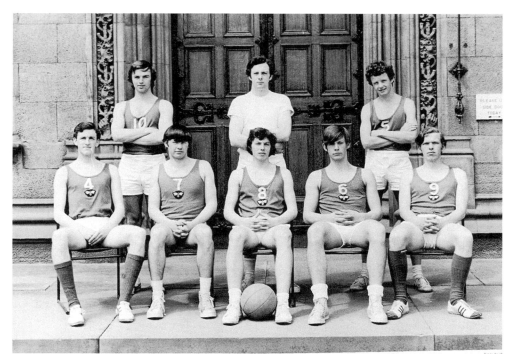

Early steps in leadership: Tony Blair (seated centre) captains the basketball team in 1971.

Amanda Mackenzie-Stuart, the first girl to be admitted to Fettes in 1970, presents the Queen Mother with a bouquet.

your contemporaries at foreign universities – riot!' The argument was the same as Edinburgh citizens had used in 1883. In his autobiography Ogilvy records: 'This was greeted with loud and prolonged applause from the boys and the following year Fettes went co-ed.' In reality it was not quite so simple. In 1969 a request came in from Lansdowne House School. Three girls wanted to take science A-levels, for which the School had neither provision or lab space. Could they join the Fettes Upper Sixth for their classes? McIntosh (not slow to appreciate the special dimension girls can bring to a class) was quick to respond, so the girls appeared for each class in taxis, which then swept them off at the end lest togetherness extend beyond the class-room. There was no time for friendships to develop, but a tiny breach had been made in the wall of masculinity. 'Co-education has reared its ugly head,' said McIntosh at Centenary Founder's Day. But by then he had taken a much bigger step. After a good lunch on the previous year's Founder's Day, one of his Governors, Jack Mackenzie-Stuart, raised with him over the second brandy the problem of his daughter Amanda. The Wiltshire boarding school she was attending was first-rate, but she was tired of boarding and desperate to be a day-girl at home in Edinburgh for the Sixth Form. Could McIntosh take her the following September? To Jack's surprise, McIntosh replied: 'I don't see why not. I'll talk to the Governors.' When Jack followed this up with a letter, McIntosh responded positively and the deed was done. Amanda entered the School as the single girl pupil in September 1970. Outnumbered in a ratio of 440 to 1, she valiantly took on the challenge, but was relieved when a friend joined her at half-term, and so it grew. The staff with one or two exceptions were delighted, and in 1971 Kate Eveling was appointed as the first female member of the full-time staff.

In spite of this pioneering move, Ian McIntosh's final years at Fettes were less than happy. He hated the endless questioning and the niggles over long hair, and reacted by becoming ever more defensive. Although the boys saw him simply as the man who stopped them doing the things their non-boarding friends were doing, he felt resented. The housemasters were finding him too inflexible, and there were financial worries. There was an over-run of £40,000 on the dining hall, and although sales of land had brought in a total of £350,000, expenditure of £380,000 on non-Appeal improvements like upgrading the houses and building the Science School meant a further deficit of £30,000. The income and expenditure account had gone into the red to the tune of more than £100,000, and the general fund of the Fettes Trust now stood at only £37,000. The question had to be asked whether the Governors had not been too slow to raise fees. The numbers were not yet high enough to remedy the situation even though the capacity of the School had risen with the building of Arniston. They had stayed at or above the figure of 459 inherited from Crichton-Miller until the mid-1960s, when they slipped by around 20 – a drop which probably reflects McIntosh's distaste for PR. When he left they stood at 436, but the academic 'hurdle' had to be lowered to keep numbers up. In his last year he had to mount a second appeal to modernise studies and dormitories in College, make the swimming pool all-weather and create a new waiting house. Just when the School needed good will, Crichton-Miller himself wrote an open letter to Alan Waddell in the summer of 1971 criticising the Governors and what he saw as the School's failure in marketing. The Governors were furious with Crichton-Miller's assumption of the role of adviser to his successors, and at his 'inaccurate' and unconstructive letter. But its contents circulated among the old boys and helped to undermine the Appeal. At the same time the rugby-minded Old Fettesians, who had seen Crichton-Miller (OF and rugby cap) as 'one of them' and had never been sure about McIntosh's regime, were up in arms at the abandonment of double fixtures. The days when only a limited number of local schools could match Fettes on the rugby field were past, and the coaches were keen to take on schools like Heriot's, Dollar and Stewart's, who were now producing fine teams. This meant playing the old rivals only once a year, an idea repugnant to such OFs. McIntosh accepted his coaches' view, in which the rival schools concurred, and the change was made in 1971.

McIntosh's critics pointed out his inflexibility, the authoritarian, over-centralised style, the puritanism and the narrow range of his innovations. But against these were ranged great strengths. A fine teacher, he kept a strong emphasis on academic performance and was excellent at choosing staff, so that ten of his appointees became headmasters, several with immense distinction. He was a brilliant public speaker, with a keen wit and a sharp mind that went quickly to the heart of any discussion. Honest and unmercenary, with a clear sense of right and wrong based on his Christian beliefs, he stayed true to the standards of his Highland youth, and though his last years were an ordeal, he came through battered but unbowed. He had kept control by a refusal to let his principles bend before the wind of change.

Ian McIntosh in 1971.

The very consistency and loyalty to his beliefs which seemed like obstinacy to some were to others his greatest virtue.

The end of his period of office brought consolations. The visit of Her Majesty's Inspectorate in 1970 produced a glowing report, and 16 Fettesians gained entry to Oxbridge. The rugby, hockey and cricket teams were winning again, and the Centenary with its building programme was a tremendous success. At the end of the Centenary Commem dinner, after an extraordinary and over-long speech by Donald Crichton-Miller criticising (among others) the Governors for financial mis-management, Ian McIntosh rose at midnight to a standing ovation from the Old Fettesians who had been at school in his time. Discarding great chunks of his pre-pared speech, he distilled his message to the old boys into five minutes with immense panache and wit. At the end the whole hall rose to him. It was a sweet moment, when so many who cheered had chafed under his regime as pupils. He had intended to retire in 1970, but at the Governors' request he stayed on until 1971. At his last Founder's Day, he spoke humbly, thanking the boys for their tol-erance: 'In so far as the Headmaster is the man who is paid to say "no", members of the School probably feel that I have been only too conscientious in the pursuit of my duty.' At the end of his last term there was another sweet moment, as a farewell concert in honour of Ian and Florence, who had backed him up with so much hard work, quiet charm and concern for the staff wives, ended with Ian sit-ting relaxed on the stage reading the delighted boys a poem he had composed him-self. The avuncular figure was a McIntosh they had all too seldom seen. The need always to act up to the *persona* of Headmaster had been a constant strain, and one could speculate that he might have been happier, with his incisive mind and superb delivery, as perhaps Professor of Languages at a great Scottish University. As it was, the 1960s were over, he and his school had survived, and he had served her well.

An aerial view of the School estate, looking south.

7

Taking the Lid Off
CHENEVIX-TRENCH : 1971–79

The small, remarkable man who arrived in the summer of 1971 was the fourth English classicist to become Headmaster of Fettes, but in other ways was an unlikely choice. Tony Chenevix-Trench had no Scottish links apart from the Chair in Greek at Edinburgh University occupied by his great-uncle, and he cut a very different figure from his predecessor. He came armed with an extraordinary *curriculum vitae*. A classicist and a schoolboy at Shrewsbury like Potts, he also had two short spells teaching there. His undergraduate career at Christ Church, Oxford, was interrupted by the war, when he spent three and a half years as a prisoner of the Japanese at Changi and on the Burma railway. Returning to Oxford, he gained a remarkable first, and after a taste of teaching at his old school, went back to Christ Church as a don. Missing the boys and visualizing himself 'getting pickled in port', he stayed only a year and then went back as housemaster to Shrewsbury, before becoming in succession Headmaster of Bradfield and Eton, where he 'felt like a donkey entered for the Derby.' Suddenly, in 1970, he was looking for a job.

Popularly thought to have resigned from Eton out of frustration at conservative resistance to his reforms ('My Provost and I,' he had written to his brother, 'have very different ideas. His ethics, as you may say, are utilitarian, mine Kantian.'), he was later declared (notably in 1994 by Tim Card in *Eton Renewed*) to have been asked to leave because of administrative weaknesses and fondness for the bottle and the cane. In 1969, two boys he had expelled went straight to the offices of *Private Eye*, staffed largely, as luck would have it, by men he had beaten at Shrewsbury in their schooldays. The upshot was an article by Paul Foot, 'Jolly Beating Weather', asserting that Trench enjoyed beating.

When the Fettes Governors were trawling the field for a successor to McIntosh, they seem to have been quite unaware of these problems. McIntosh had visited Eton and Phil Macpherson had spoken to Lord Caccia, diplomat and Provost of Eton, but no hostile noises from any source were reported to the Governors. At Eton, the official story was still that Trench had left the school because of incompatibility, but at Fettes, though one or two had misgivings, the Governors' pleasure at finding the Headmaster of Eton on their list, his performance at interview and

Tony Chenevix-Trench in 1971.

the lack of any other strong candidate (perhaps because the salary on offer was so low) apparently did not incline them to look too deeply into the background to his sudden departure from Eton.

Tony Trench arrived in August 1971 at a school still reverberating with the battles of the age of revolt and short of ready cash, but fundamentally in good shape. Though he puzzlingly described it later as 'a sinking school of 392 boys', it in fact numbered 436. Less traumatic times were at hand for public schools. The struggles over authority that had shattered their equilibrium were set to ebb gradually over the early 1970s and, with the loosening of the old hierarchies, leave in their wake genuine improvements to make up for all the aggravation – a decline in bullying and homosexuality, and improved staff–pupil relationships. Trench's personality fitted this climate, and his arrival seemed at once to lighten the atmosphere. The hierarchies which, for McIntosh, were the crucial props of an ordered society meant little to Trench. He had egalitarian tendencies, possibly strengthened by his gruesome experiences on the Burma railway, where rank had little to do with how prisoners coped with the conditions. He hated élitism and was unimpressed with power. When he had just moved in to the Headmaster's lodge, Harry Headspeath, school handyman, came to deliver initial supplies. Taking off his jacket, Trench helped Harry heave the boxes into the lodge and then brought him into the kitchen for a beer and a chat. It was a new style for a Fettes Headmaster. His habit of puncturing his own dignity (in so far as it existed) had already shocked housemasters at Eton, when third-formers returned from his house with tales of having played 'Are you there, Moriarty?' on the floor with the Headmaster. Young and vulnerable boys were particularly important to him, and when the Fettes 'new men' arrived for tea at the start of term he would seek out the shyest to talk to and reassuringly stuff their pockets with chocolate biscuits. Staff were all told 'Call me Tony'.

The apotheosis of Trench's democratic style was perhaps 'the knees-up' – a Christmas party he started at the end of his first term for everyone employed on the campus. The first of these was a sticky occasion. At one end of the room stood housemasters' wives nervously sipping sherry while at the other beer was being cheerfully drunk by the other ranks, sitting on benches. The clash of protocols looked unpromising, until Trench resorted to party tricks like lying flat on his back in the middle and balancing a tumbler of water on his forehead (not to show off, but to break the all-too-obvious ice), before asking George Lindsay to sing 'You'll Never Walk Alone' and then leading Hilda, the Carrington cleaner, onto the floor for a St Bernard's waltz. He had a wonderful asset in his wife Elizabeth, who won all hearts, keeping an eye on staff children, starting 'The Monday Club' for staff wives and matrons, and providing the girls with cookery classes and a shoulder to cry on. Her special combination of dignity and warmth was something rare. Another of Trench's powerful assets was his humane Second Master Dick Cole-Hamilton, who shared his liberal values but kept the school administration firmly on the rails.

A month into his first term, Trench reported to the Governors that he intended to relax discipline. 'Fettes has acquired a reputation, especially in the south, as a very tough school,' he told them. He would try to deal with boys one-to-one. He placed great faith in self-discipline, and saw the teens as 'a conscious progress from the must to the ought.' Rules had their place. 'Who would plant a sapling in windy Fettes without first tying it to a stake in the early years to preserve it from being broken by the gales?' he asked. Adolescents, he knew, would be sinners, not saints, but, as Dick Cole-Hamilton put it, he wanted them to be 'sinners with a conscience'. The picture of Trench as a sadistic figure ('the Eton flogger') distilled by the media out of Card's book is at odds with the gentle way he treated young offenders. He would do anything rather than expel someone. He even sent one offender off to Alnmouth Friary to see if the friars could save him from himself. His disciplinary talks were worlds away from the style of his predecessors. After one lecture to the school, he finished: 'I'm so sorry to be cross with you, my dears, but don't let it ever happen again.' He gave sixth-formers leave out into the city on any Saturday evening until 11 p.m. He was intensely bored by matters of dress, and relaxed rules on turn-out, seeming hardly to notice long hair and permitting boots (then in fashion) as well as shoes, though if people got too untidy, he might gently remonstrate with them in their reports: 'Buck up, old thing!', 'Please try to look less as if you had been pulled half-asleep out of a hay-stack,' or 'It really only needs a bit of woad to make Colin look like an adolescent ancient Briton.' The liberal stance of the Headmaster was now at odds with the conservatism of some prefects. Trench contented himself with indicating his own dislike of things like personal fagging, but leaving housemasters to act as each saw fit. Manners, though, were a priority. 'Manners,' he said in one Founder's Day speech, 'are the happy way of

The fourteen girls at Fettes in 1975.

99

doing things. Some of you may say that they are superficial, but so are the dew drops that give such depth and beauty to the morning meadow.'

The early results of the Chenevix-Trench era were gratifying. The Oxford and Cambridge results, which had surged ahead in McIntosh's last year, held up strongly, with six awards in Trench's first year and eight in his second (as well as 15 places). Only twice in the 1970s did the number of places gained fall below double figures. Science, with its fine new building, was set to gain in status under successive heads of science David Rhodes and David Kennedy, and the Art Room was pulsating with life as John Brown built on the work of his gifted predecessors. The recruitment of clever girls into the Sixth Form gave a boost to academic performance, and the change in 1972 from a Form system to a Tutorial system refined the process of supervision. Academic success was becoming ever more important to public schools in the 1970s, as, in the delicate financial climate, parents above all wanted value for money, which meant good exam results. Nor did games results falter, and by 1973 the first three XVs and the Senior Colts were all unbeaten. In 1974, a palpitating rugby victory over the unbeaten touring team from Llandovery electrified the spectators in a way which recalled the gladiatorial fixtures of the past. When Fettes were trailing 10 - 6, a skein of geese flew over Bigside, and Trench, noting that they flew in from the right, announced to Nick Ridley the coach that, according to the Roman science of augury, this meant a win for the home team. So it proved, with a converted try in the final minute.

One piece of unfinished business that Trench had inherited from McIntosh was the proposed reopening of the junior (waiting) house in Malcolm House and the old Sanatorium. In no time at all, Trench had bigger ideas. 'I left him a goose egg,' McIntosh was to say, 'and he turned it into an ostrich egg.' In his first term, Trench proposed to the Governors that, instead of a waiting house, it should open as a separate Junior School for up to 80 boys, bridging the gap between the end of primary school and Fettes' traditional entry at 13. 'Prep school headmasters,' he reported to the Governors on 16th November 1971, 'had indicated that such a school would not be in competition with them.' This assertion was to be sorely tested in years to come. By 3rd October 1972, the Governors had decided to go ahead with the Junior School, which became the major initiative of the Trench era. It would be a day school, though 'in appropriate cases' boys could board with masters' families. To qualify for entry to the main school, boys would have to pass the same Common Entrance exam as boys from prep schools. John Arkell, head of English, was appointed its first Headmaster, and he and his wife Jean proved ideal for the challenge. With their wide circle of Edinburgh friends, they soon put the Junior School on the map. It opened in September 1973 and the numbers had already reached 80 by January 1975. But the trouble with the way it was set up was its incompatibility with the Senior School. When one was a day school and the other boarding, there was bound to be pressure in the future for the Junior School to take boarders (bringing it into unwelcome rivalry with prep schools) and for the Senior School to take day boys. This was just what happened. The admission of day boys into the Senior School was rejected by the Governors in May 1974, but only eight months later they decided that 20 could be accepted on a 'highly selective' basis. Fourteen months later the school started planning for 'a considerable expansion in day boy numbers'. Part of the thinking behind this *volte-face* was economic. By 1976 inflation was running at 25 per cent per annum, and Trench thought this trend would erode the capital of the professional classes, making the future uncertain for boarding schools. This scenario was not realised to any drastic degree. The boarding market declined gently rather than collapsing immediately, and there was merely a steady growth in the number of day boys. More damaging was the prep school headmasters' sense of betrayal. They were sensitive anyway about the signs of decline in their sector, and as boarding built up in the Junior School, they saw Trench's assurances that it would not tap into their market as double-talk, and started retaliating in the only way open to them, by directing their pupils to other schools.

Up till now, Trench had been highly successful in recruiting pupils. The number of boarding boys inherited from McIntosh was sustained, and he added to it day boys and more Sixth Form girls. By 1974, as the girl entry built up, there were around 60–70 applicants for 17 places per year. Total numbers in the School rose from 428 in 1972 to 525 by 1978, with 84 in the Junior School. Several houses had to resort to bunk beds to fit everyone in. Trench was at his best with prospective parents, making them at home in his own drawing-room and seizing a chance for a *tête-à-tête* with their son or daughter as soon as the prospective housemaster arrived to join them. For many a boy, the interview ordeal was softened by the way Trench took such interest in his enthusiasms, or showed him some treasure like his tray of polished stones. He had told the Governors that 'slower developers contribute more,' which had the ring of a warning that he would be admitting boys with low Common Entrance marks. Certainly, not all staff were happy with some boys who found their way into the School. 'Don't let the Housemaster see that file,' he would say of a dubious entrant's past record. If the file did get through, he would sugar the pill by assuring the Housemaster that he was uniquely fitted to give a problem pupil the best chance of success.

The number of girls crept steadily upwards. After the Governors at Marlborough had allowed John Dancy to take girls into the Sixth Form in 1969, the practice spread to many other schools in the 1970s, to the understandable chagrin of the all-girl schools. Dancy had admitted them, not for economic reasons, but to 'consolidate the liberal position.' Some of the cruel or philistine features of traditional boy school life had gone into retreat before the relentless questionings of the 1960s. As girls came in with greater maturity and found boys behaving like bullies or tyrants, they tended to point this out, and it all helped to stop the barbarities of the past reappearing. Their arrival also improved master–pupil relationships. The convention in all-boy schools was to call boys by their surnames, but masters could not bring themselves to do this with girls, and the resultant inconsistency meant that soon boys' Christian names were in use too. There was, of course, the danger that masters unused to teaching girls would over-indulge them. Many were quite unsure how to treat them, especially if they were ever out of line.

To Trench, who had never taught girls, the two he had inherited from McIntosh

Above: Trial by Jury, *1962.*
With no girls yet, bride and
bridesmaids are played by boys.
Note the left-hand bridesmaid's
reluctance to be photographed in
'her' outfit.
Above right: *in 1972, John*
Arkell conducts a rehearsal for
Antigone with a mixed cast,
aiming for increased naturalism.

were an enigma. 'I remember the first time a girl was sent to me for misbehaving,' he said later. 'We were both very nervous and eventually burst into helpless giggles. I said, "Well, Amanda darling, just clear out, old thing, and don't ever darken my study door again."' Like other heads, though, he knew that many of the girls would be hard-working and clever, especially as demand built up and outstripped the number of places available. Having begun with 'a toe in the water' – a single girl in 1970 – Fettes was to have 40 girls by 1979. Like all Sixth Form girl entrants to public schools, they had to get used to the chauvinistic antics of the boys and having their attractions categorised on arrival. This could be an ordeal at any school and lead to unhappiness for plain or unacademic girls. At Fettes they could seem, in Trench's phrase, like 'a limpet clinging to a Scottish masculine rock', but one, Amynta Wood-Gush, later told a *Guardian* journalist: 'For me, Fettes was bliss from start to finish. I felt desperately special.'

Boy–girl problems never ran ostentatiously out of control, and no couples were found *flagrante delicto*, although methods of detection were probably far from perfect. Girls were an asset to many activities like drama, reducing the need for boy actresses, where in former days, according to Roddy Macdonald, 'an agile, but macho scrum-half would, with grease paint, wig and two judiciously inserted grapefruit, blossom into a bouncy Restoration trollop.' It was good to say good-bye to such suspension of disbelief. By 1975, at a debate attended by around 200, a motion that 'This House believes that the introduction of girls has been a disaster' was defeated by a massive majority. 'The girls are huge fun,' said Trench, 'and I think they help civilise the place.' The first girls were attached to Glencorse, then to Carrington and then, as numbers grew, to other houses. But since the School had started with one girl, no-one had really got down to dictating their life-style by any formal structure, and some boys resented the way they dressed as they liked ('draw-string T-shirts, loons and platform soles') and seemed to inhabit a separate discipli-nary world. In 1975 the need for a girls' 'minder' was realised, and Marie Simmons took on the job. By December 1978, a school poll showed that 56 per cent of the school would like to see all-through co-education. Only 25 per cent of the girls themselves were for it, though; they seem to have treasured their exclusivity. When George Mathewson, Headmaster of nearby prep school Clifton Hall, asked one of his ex-pupils what he thought of co-education at Fettes, he got the reply: 'It's great. It keeps the prefects' minds off the likes of us.'

Two major weaknesses of the Chenevix-Trench era were poor staff appoint-ments (with the odd shining exception) and a failure to improve the plant. Trench never took enough trouble over appointments, and often went simply on personal recommendation or took someone who happened to write in offering their services. His interview technique was cavalier in the extreme, and candidates were often sub-jected to a long monologue. Ian Winstanley, one of his appointees, claims to have made only one remark during his entire interview for a job. It was: 'I believe you've dropped your pipe.' References weren't always followed up, and some of his appointments stored up trouble for his successor.

The girls join CCF: the Annual Inspection of 1983.

The failure of the School to develop its buildings in the 1970s let Fettes get behind its rivals in terms of facilities. The author remembers the ordeal of con-ducting parents in the late 1970s round Carrington House where a Dickensian aura still hung around the bare floorboards and acres of dark brown varnish. An appeal to Trench for action to improve living conditions was answered by a phrase from Thucydides, meaning 'It's people who make up a community'. This was absolutely right in principle, but in effect an excuse for doing nothing. Apart from the con-version of the Junior School premises, no building projects were undertaken in his time, which elsewhere saw a tremendous surge in building in the independent sec-tor at large. The idea of moving the school, which had come up under McIntosh, reappeared with the suggestion from one Governor that Fettes should sell the school site, merge with St Leonard's and move to Hopetoun House outside Edinburgh. It was not followed up.

It is certainly true that Trench found the money problems of the 1970s agoniz-ing. This goes some way towards explaining his inaction. Plans like the merging of College East and College West were intended to make the school cheaper to run, though he persuaded the Governors that the change to study bedrooms there was essential. The new School House started in 1971 and prospered under David

Pighills, with numbers reaching 130. It continued united under Andrew Gordon Clark and Peter Coshan, but it was simply too big, and after 17 years it was to be divided once again as it filled up with girls. As steep inflation took hold, the financial problems intensified. Numbers were going up, but neither the girls nor the Junior School boys were providing boarding fees, as the ones who did board stayed with local families. The Governors were hesitant to lift the fees to compensate, as there was always the lingering dread of pricing the school out of the market.

In 1975 things came to a head with the publication of the Houghton Report. The Houghton Commission on teachers' pay prescribed a rise of 30 per cent for the state sector, backdated to May 1974. Trench and the Governors were aghast. The backdating in particular would add £18,000 to the school's overdraft, and Trench pleaded with the staff to forego it for the sake of the school, pointing out that he had asked for his own salary not to be raised. They finally agreed, but the whole episode was a cliff-hanger. He wrote to Cameron Miller on 10 May,

> Times are (truism worthy of a Greek chorus!) not easy, but those who too easily lose heart will wake to find their world as easily lost. So let us get on with it! As that old funny, Barrie, said, 'Courage is all – all goes if courage goes.' It is not the first time in our history that we have faced disaster, eyeball to eyeball.

He cancelled Founder's Day that year to economise – not a huge benefit to the overdraft but a very public statement of tight purse-strings, as well as a welcome let-off from the Founder's Day speech, always an ordeal for him. When the School desperately needed a minibus, he took the slightly impudent step of writing a direct begging letter to rich old boy David Ogilvy: 'My dear David, you are stinking rich. We need a minibus. It will cost you £7,000.' Ogilvy's reply by return was terse: 'You biscuit!' (euphemism?), but he enclosed a cheque for the sum in question. In 1976, Trench announced the formation of 'Friends of Fettes', but this was not a money-spinner, and when the Distillers' Company bid £450,000 (later raised to £550,000) for 5.3 acres of the east half of the golf course as a site for their HQ, it sounded at last as if the goose had laid a golden egg. Hopes were dashed when the Distillers' building was turned down by the City Planning Department, mainly on the grounds that it would interfere with Edinburgh's (not very attractive) northern skyline (though some thought they were reluctant to see an independent school profiting from such a deal). This meant that, for the rest of his time, Trench was always navigating murky financial waters, but he kept his head well above them thanks to the careful guidance of Alan Waddell, who took over the Governors' finance committee.

The press reaction to books on Tony Chenevix-Trench like *Eton Renewed* and *The Land of Lost Content* focused to such a degree on his taste for beating and drink that his pastoral gifts were understressed. He was closer to the boys than any other Fettes headmaster, and none saw him as the sadistic beater of legend. At his first assembly in 1971, he told the school that 'my study door is always open to those who want to see me,' and he meant it. 'Never turn a boy away,' he said once to his secretary Gracie Gavin when she told one visitor that the Headmaster was too busy to see him. An innocent new 13-year-old arrival in 1977, Brookes Poole, was put up by his friends to ringing the Headmaster's doorbell as they watched from the

The notice on Chenevix-Trench's Study door, demonstrating his resolve always to be accessible to his pupils.

IF NOTICE SAYS 'OUT' AND YOU WANT TO SEE ME, GO TO LODGE (DO NOT RING), ENTER HALL, TRY FIRST DOOR ON RIGHT. — MY STUDY. FAILING TO GET ME THERE, LEAVE NOTE OF NAME AND HOUSE IN HALL AND I'LL ARRANGE EARLIEST APPtment ACT

bushes outside. Imagining a flunkey would answer and that he could talk his way out of it, Brookes was aghast when his Headmaster opened the door. Improvising wildly, he came up with the extraordinary remark (since he lived in France): 'Last holiday I visited the gardens at Versailles, and now I'd like to see round yours.' One can imagine the reaction of most headmasters to this opening, but without a pause Trench came out and showed him patiently round the whole garden, and then took him inside for coffee and biscuits. After they'd talked for some time, he said 'Well, I think you'd better be going now. Your friends out there will be getting cold.'

'To Mr Chenevix-Trench,' said one of his heads of school, 'every boy in this School is the only boy in the School.' He was in effect counsellor to the School, and although this could be abused and the territorial sense of some housemasters was offended, he rescued a number of potential drop-outs. He loved to fight, alongside them, the traumas of puberty. He saw it as a tunnel, and in one boy's report he wrote: 'Probably he has just entered the tunnel of the Ghost Train at the Adolescent Fair.' There was always light at the other end. 'Youth is short, so it does matter whether it is spent happily or not.' Because he was so much loved by the boys and girls, they made light of the way he beat or the times when he seemed to have been drinking, putting quirks of behaviour down to his war experiences. The root cause of his fondness for the cane remains unclear, as Mark Peel's diagnosis in his biography acknowledges. The fact that when he beat a boy he first asked whether he agreed with the punishment and afterwards treated him with great courtesy suggests it was a compulsion that satisfied one side of his personality but offended another. After beating a boy involved in minor mayhem during the early hours of the last night of one summer term, he took him into his kitchen and cooked him breakfast.

By around 1977, the excellent image of the School which the Headmaster's popularity and good academic and games performance had created was being undermined as reports of boys out of school, untidily dressed or drinking at strange hours spread in Edinburgh. In March 1977 the *Evening News* and one or two national newspapers reported a small number of Fettesians being fined in an Edinburgh court for under-age drinking. The problem was a mixture of Trench's relaxation of the leave-out rules and the growth in the number of day pupils. The problems within the boarding community of compatibility with the freedoms of, especially, day girls, caused tensions and the taking of liberties. 'As you and I can see,' wrote a candid sixth-former to Trench in July 1977, 'the School's standard is going down. It is not you who is to blame, but the whole community.' The relaxation of discipline, which had seemed so right in 1971, was generating a *laissez-faire* attitude, and housemasters found that referring wrongdoers to the Headmaster was not much of a deterrent. Boarding numbers started to dip sharply. After reaching an all-time high of 487 in 1977, they were down to 448 the following year, with some weak applicants being admitted. Bad publicity was compounded by the growing suspicion of the Junior School in prep schools, and occasions when Trench went ahead with public speeches when unfit to do so. His health was declining, and since his one-to-one disciplinary system depended so much on him personally, this further undermined it. The anaesthetic for his 'tummy ache' (the failure of his liver, originally damaged by protein deficiency at Changi) was drink. 'The doctor says I should give up whisky,' he told Cameron Miller. 'I've taken a considered view. The quality of life is more important than the quantity.' After putting up a notice one day in 1978 saying that he would be away from school for 24 hours, he told Cameron that in fact he was going to bed with a bottle of whisky and 'hoping the pain would go away.'

Administration was often inconsistent, and he failed to prod staff enough when things were clearly getting lax. As in the past, he would make promises to members of staff which he couldn't fulfil. At housemasters' meetings, Trench often changed the subject when a contentious issue was raised. Growing absent-mindedness led to awkward episodes, as when the swimming bath was full of policemen and their wives and he went in to join them, forgetting to put his swimming trunks on first. Used to his own failings, Trench had developed a gift for turning aside angry reactions. When Margaret Buchanan-Smith wrote him a blistering letter about inconsistent discipline, his reply began: 'Darling Margaret, how wonderful that you feel able to write to me so freely!' On 2nd February 1978, he was rushed to hospital with severe internal haemorrhaging, and the Governors asked Dick Cole-Hamilton to act in his place until the summer term. They also persuaded Trench to announce his retirement as from August 1979. He would be 60 by then, but had been keen to stay longer.

His last year was a happier and more relaxed one. In May he wrote to Mary Davidson,

> I shall be sad to retire from my best loved school in August, but at 60+ I know it is right. I hope God will grant me a few more years of teaching – anywhere, boys or girls, for I love it. Anyway, Deo Gratias! I've had a full and happy life.

The staff in 1979. Sitting down, from left to right, are Tom Goldie-Scot, Mike Leslie, Chevenix-Trench (with Scampi) and Ian Sutcliffe.

In his last term he gave a series of media interviews appropriate to an *eminence grise* of the profession. 'All you need with a child,' he told the *Evening News* 'is firmness and affection. The affection must be absolutely constant and you must never let him down.' In a typical act of thoughtfulness, he rang up British Airways in May 1979 when he heard that Richard Humble was flying across the Atlantic for the first time. Humble, now aged 89, was the Fettesian who in 1932 had taught himself to fly in South Africa, and flown a bi-plane back home to Glasgow via Fettes, in order to swoop down to 100 feet above the cricketers on Turf and drop a note of greeting to Pyatt, his old Housemaster. Now, half way across the Atlantic in 1979, the pilot of the jumbo jet called for Humble and asked him to take over the controls. The delighted Humble never knew who had fixed it for him.

Trench's *credo* was delivered to the parents with a characteristic excess of modesty at his last Founder's Day on 2 June 1979. He admitted that he had been 'had for a sucker' in his time, through believing boys. But that was the way you make gentlemen in the long run. If they had avoided punishment, at least they had felt uncomfortable and not offended much more. They must learn to choose and not abdicate their responsibility to rule-based government. 'I have loved Fettes more than any of my former three schools,' he concluded. 'I rather think I am a fool, but I've been a happy one, rewarded beyond my deserts.' Utterly exhausted by the strain of the day, he was found in the evening by the groundsman curled up on a seat by the pavilion and helped home. Nineteen days later he was rushed into hospital after a recurrence of his old trouble, and died after an emergency operation. He was just 60. His death left the School population stunned. As the news filtered out, a young boy flung open the door of the Lodge and rushed in, screaming 'Where is he? It can't be true.' That night housemasters announced the news in bewildered silence, while the thoughts of some went back to the touching epitaph he had chosen for himself at Founder's Day three weeks earlier, from G. K. Chesterton's 'Ballad of the White Horse', words of the Saxon thane Eldred before his death, fighting for Alfred against the Danes at Ethandune:

A caricature of Chenevix-Trench by David Jackson Young, 1976.

> The kings go up and the kings go down,
> And who knows who shall rule,
> But men and birds and dogs may weep
> At the burial of a fool.
>
> O, lodgers in my cellar,
> Boys in my apple trees,
> The world grows stern and strange and new,
> And wiser men shall govern you,
> Yet some fools weep for me.

And not just fools either.

Autumn on the rugby field in the 1980s.

8

The Girls Move In
COCHRANE : 1979–88

Tony Chenevix-Trench's widow Elizabeth bravely did the honours at the final leave-taking after Dick Cole-Hamilton had acted again as Headmaster for the last two weeks of the summer term of 1979. A year earlier the Governors had appointed as Tony's successor Cameron Cochrane, whom many of them knew already. Cochrane, a product of the Edinburgh Academy and Headmaster of Arnold School, Blackpool, had been an assistant director of education in Edinburgh, and the governors felt he would be at home with the mushrooming bureaucracy of education and would also use his Edinburgh connections to improve the School's local image – though ironically he was to have less success than Trench in wooing the local 'mafia'. His wife Rosemary brought great modesty and charm to her role as Headmaster's wife and hostess at the Lodge, winning the affection of the community.

He did not inherit an easy job. The drop in the birth-rate was already affecting prep school numbers, and secondary schools were about to experience a 30 per cent drop. Within the School, the demand for boys' boarding places had started to decline as its reputation in the local community and the prep schools deteriorated. Classrooms and boarding houses were looking run-down, and, behind the façade of Oxbridge success, performance in public examinations was very patchy. In Trench's last years, it had been easy for senior Fettesians to drink in the city's pubs, which were too numerous to be easy to patrol. A tragic symptom of this was the death of a sixth-former in Cochrane's first term. Andy Campbell, a delightful and popular member of School House, was asphyxiated climbing into College in the early hours of Sunday 14th October. It was a traumatic start.

Cochrane could see at once that urgent action was needed to secure numbers. Encouraged by the Governors, he launched an immediate survey of the School's current strengths and weaknesses in consultation with staff, and set out a range of options for the future. His analysis made clear his strong support for full co-education, amounting to a 'clear vision'. Some Governors were in favour, though others were less easy to convince. Some of the Old Fettesians among them shrank from the implications, the spectre of lacrosse rivalling rugby on the games fields, the enormity of the change involved in the character of the School. Others, by contrast, agreed with Cochrane that co-education was in keeping with the *zeitgeist* and saw beyond the economic advantages to those expressed by John Buchanan, Head of Oakham School (quoted by John Rae):

> The hobbledehoy masculinity of a boys' school, which is so often accompanied by an undue emphasis on competitive games and an absence of social compassion, is at once muted in a co-educational school . . . Essentially a school should be co-educational because education should prepare for life . . . The simple lesson which a monosex school learns on becoming co-educational is the rediscovery of a relaxed normality; one is no longer struggling to operate an inherently abnormal community.

Early in Cochrane's second year, the Governors took the plunge, and on 21st November 1980 parents and members of the School were told that the Senior School was to welcome girls in the 13–18 age range from September 1983, that the Junior School would become co-educational from September 1981, and that Arniston was to be converted to become the first girls' boarding house in 1983. Far the youngest house, it had, as a result, relatively few former members to complain at its sex-change. It was also slightly apart, and easily convertible into the study bedrooms girls might expect. Jean, wife of the Chaplain, David Weekes, who had already been looking after the girls, would be the first Housemistress. After the announcement, applications from girls grew rapidly, and Cochrane was soon planning for a second girls' house, to be opened in 1984. School House was selected because it was secure and could expand or contract according to demand, allowing unneeded space to be used for teaching or offices.

David Clark with Junior School girls and boys, in 1990.

In neither Arniston nor School House, however, was the change-over trouble-free. The boys who had to move to another house were not always well prepared for the change, and some former members of School House, a bastion of masculinity for 114 years, were vociferous in their disapproval. For one year, School House boys and girls co-existed in a tolerant atmosphere before Peter Coshan withdrew and the remaining boys were scattered, leaving Margot Rawson in charge as Housemistress, until she left in 1988 and the House was again divided into two. Day girls now had a new house created for them, Dalmeny, which in 1984 took up residence in the west ground floor of College. The gender revolution was matched on the governing body, where the first two women Governors, Mary Corsar and Kay Kemball, were appointed in 1982.

The Junior School day boy numbers meanwhile were dropping. The Governors had wondered whether to close it down (arriving at an 'arrangement' with two local prep schools) or provide proper boarding facilities. The second option was pushed hard by David Clark, its young new Headmaster, and by 1982 it was agreed to build a new boarding wing. For years some Junior School boys had effectively been boarders, lodging with members of staff, and it was a logical step to house these together on the spot. But the prep school heads were indignant that what Trench had assured them was a day school was now quite obviously a boarding establishment, and did nothing to encourage their pupils to choose Fettes.

In the climate of the early 1980s, what parents wanted was value for money, which increasingly meant academic success. Oxford and Cambridge universities were under pressure to admit fewer products of public schools and were making tougher demands on candidates, which injected new urgency into the academic side of school life. If results were to be lifted, co-ordination and forward planning were called for, and in September 1980 Cochrane created the post of Director of Studies and appointed Michael McIntosh Reid. The two-track Sixth Form curriculum, headed towards a choice of English A-levels or Scottish Highers, was given a better defined structure, in a pattern that was imitated by other 'mixed economy' Scottish schools. Another new appointment, designed to sharpen up day-to-day behaviour and discipline, was that of Proctor, and Australian Neville Clark made an immediate impact in this role, with his air of command and readiness to grasp nettles. George Preston, the newly appointed Senior Master, tackled, with his help, problems like the chaotic bottleneck before lunch, rapidly restoring order and dignity to the dining hall. Meanwhile in 1981 Mike O'Callaghan was appointed Steward and overhauled the whole economy of Fettes food.

The year 1981 was a worrying one. Boarding numbers were declining just when funds were needed to build a boarding extension to the Junior School and convert Arniston for girls. The non-boarding Junior School was now down to 61. It was a difficult time for many schools. They looked anxiously round at one another, their sympathy for a neighbour in trouble tinged by a touch of *schadenfreude*, when they might feel with La Rochefoucauld: 'In the misfortunes of our best friends we find something which is not displeasing to us.' The new Head of Merchiston Castle School, a local rival which in the 1970s had looked to be heading for the rocks,

Cochrane with Stephen Baker, Head of School, 1987.

took time out to start with a charm offensive on the local prep schools. The Governors pressed Cochrane to do more active recruiting, but the fact was that prep school boarding numbers were dropping off sharply. Cochrane did not enjoy selling Fettes boarding to them. He knew his boarding accommodation was below par, and he was conscious that Trench's launching of the Junior School and his own plans to expand it made for uneasy dialogue with prep school heads. However, he had an imaginative video made which was sent round the world and stirred up interest in places like Hong Kong and Europe, and formed links with schools in Canada, the States and Australia.

There were other concerns, apart from the worries about recruitment. Most staff found Cochrane easy to talk to and receptive to their ideas, but there was a limit to his patience when he thought people were blocking necessary changes. The exam pass rates that summer (56 per cent at O-level and 68 per cent at A-level) were at a low ebb, and the SED Inspection in October contained criticisms of individual teachers and departments, suggesting that the weak areas needed closer monitoring. Some Labour politicians were now hinting at actual abolition of the independent sector if they regained power. Things looked discouraging all round, and the Governors were uneasy. At least the rugby was going well, though, and the XV had a fine season. By the following year they were 'arguably the best school side in Scotland.'

The fee-paying parts of the population were beginning to prosper under the Thatcher government, and during the next few years skilful footwork was needed to take the best advantage of the boom while it lasted. Day schools were flourishing,

Facing page: *a summer afternoon on Turf.*

One of the last steeplechases through the pond, 1986.

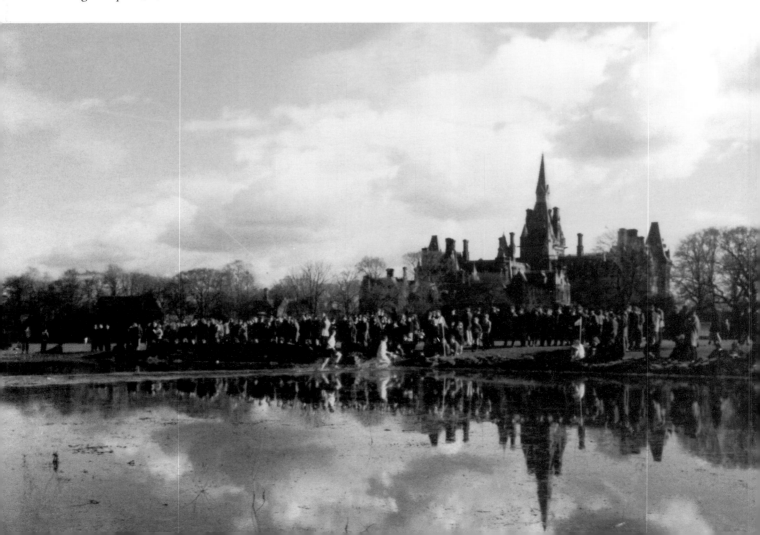

The East Drive in summer

but boarding numbers went on declining slowly. As the Government's grip was tightened in 1982 by the outcome of the war in the Falklands, the School was riveted by one of the last events of the conflict, when Fettesian Robert Lawrence of the Scots Guards led his platoon triumphantly to the top of Mount Tumbledown only to be hit by a high-velocity bullet. Sadly injured, he was given the MC and became the subject of a controversial television play.

Cochrane and the Governors meanwhile identified a number of acute building needs. A fresh appeal and the sale of land seemed the only ways to finance them. Some Old Fettesians were worried about bits of land going from the estate ('selling the family silver'), but the Governors (with exceptions) were agreeable if the terms were right and the land could be spared. When Balfour Beatty offered £710,000 for a discreet development on 5 acres of the east section of the golf course, the deal was clinched, and at the same time the small paddock behind 98, Inverleith Place was sold for the compact residential block called College View. On Founder's Day 1983, a new appeal called Fettes 2000 was launched. The Governors were advised to appeal for £600,000, but insisted on going for £1,000,000. In the end, only £460,000 was raised. Many rich Old Fettesians failed to dip into their pockets. They disapproved of the School taking girls all through, and were put off by the reports of poor discipline that had been dogging the School's reputation since the late 1970s. The proceeds were, in the end, used to modernise the Concert Hall, to expand the Art Department and set up a new Ceramics Room, to create a Sixth Form Common Room, to modernise heating, lighting and furniture in house studies and cubicles, and to extend computer facilities to the College building.

As the appeal faltered, the sale of land became crucial. By 1987 Cochrane was pushing for urgent action on the old boarding houses. New arrivals on the staff like Neil Henderson and David Burns had expressed horror at the living conditions, as did the non-Fettesian and women Governors to whom such surroundings did not represent their childhood. Mothers of prospective pupils were a new power, and, when confronted with iron bedsteads and bare boards on the floors, over-rode their husbands' nostalgia for their own schooldays and shifted their custom to schools where comfort was to be found. The Governors finally agreed that the state of Carrington, Moredun and Glencorse was putting parents off and accelerating the haemorrhage of boarding pupils. When McCarthy and Stone offered £2.9 million in early 1988 for 13 acres of the running track area, it was more than the Governors had expected. The decision was a hard one, but vital for the School's future. Without this injection of capital, the living conditions would have remained primitive and unappetizing. The Governors accepted the offer, which was well-timed. The property boom was soon over, and as interest rates soared, the School could benefit from 8–10 per cent on the £2.9 million until it had to be spent. When McCarthy and Stone had to sell the land on quickly to Fettes Village Ltd., this now meant a development of up to 263 town house and apartments looming over the Below Field, which was sadly more intensive than the School had anticipated.

A more discriminating culture was emerging among parents. When such immense sums were being laid out on schooling, they wanted to ensure value for

The Below Field from the north-east, with Junior School pupils in the foreground.

113

Tony Reeves' production of Jesus Christ Superstar *in 1986.*

money, which the old criteria of hearsay or the Oxbridge or rugby results could not guarantee. League tables were still in the future, but published guides were starting to come on the market, like *The Good Schools Guide*, published in 1986. This one, with its barely concealed snobbery and obsessive emphasis on the social skills of heads, was a mixed blessing. It described Cameron Cochrane as looking 'a bit like Michael Caine,' and Fettesians as 'dead ringers for the Prime of Miss Jean Brodie, both staff and pupils alike with Morningside accents to boot,' an unrecognisable verdict.

Myth-making was not confined to print, however. Cameron Cochrane was suffering a severe bout of 'dinner table blight'. The citizens of Edinburgh, with its high proportion of fee-paying schools, had long been obsessed with education and the minute distinctions of social standing it represented. 'Only a native,' wrote Ian Findlay, 'could possibly understand the complexities of status accorded to the various types of secondary school.' To simplify the complexities and guide one another through the maze of school choice, middle-class parents who gathered at the soirées of the New Town or the coffee parties of the Grange exchanged stories of schools and their heads for a pastime. These crystallized into word pictures of schools which, once sanctioned by repetition, fed upon themselves. In the 1980s, the image of Cochrane's Fettes was unfavourable. It was, in any case, a time when a city location (supposedly accessible to drugs) was a disadvantage. An incident in 1983, when five boys were expelled for a drug offence, did not help. The number of day pupils, which had reached a high of 119 in 1981, was down to 69 by 1988, though the fact that girls could now board had much to do with this. The total School numbers stayed above 500, but the number of boarding boys continued to head downwards, from 442 in 1979 to 200 in 1988, which, although a big drop was inevitable when three boys' houses had been turned over to girls, was still an unhealthy trend.

Within the School, however, the reality was different from the image. As girls became integrated at every level, new strengths were emerging. The School's work developed a competitive edge, and exam results improved steadily throughout the 1980s. At O-level (changed to GCSE in 1987), the pass rate moved up from 56 per cent in 1981 to 76 per cent in 1988, while by 1988 the A-level pass rate stood at a best-ever 95 per cent. Many departments were performing strongly, notably English, Art and the perennial Classics. The influx of girls injected new vigour into music and drama. A fuller choir and expanded orchestra drove up the standard of concerts, and drama was increasingly becoming a Fettes speciality. Musicals like John Arkell's *Guys and Dolls* in 1982 and Tony Reeves' *Jesus Christ Superstar* in 1986 were immensely popular, but straight plays like Reeves' *Amadeus* and *Twelfth Night* also set a high standard. The success of the School's debut on the Festival Fringe, Andrew Brownridge's production of Stoppard's *Dogg's Hamlet, Cahoot's Macbeth* in 1980, was to lead to a series of Fringe productions. As outdoor pursuits became more popular, School expeditions went ever farther afield. After climbing trips led by Nick Ridley to Arctic Norway and Greenland in 1982 and 1986, Denham

A Junior School orchestra practice in the 1980s. Susan Lester-Cribb conducts.

In recent years the School has undertaken a series of expeditions to such far-flung places as Siberia, Mongolia, Ecuador, Kenya, Arctic Norway, Zanskar and Switzerland, the key elements of which have been activities such as mountaineering, rafting and canoeing, as well as geographical and botanical field work. Here a Fettes party tackles the glacial field of Aktum in the Altai region of Siberia near the Mongolian border.

The relay swim of Lake Geneva in 1985, establishing a 'world record' of 24 hours, 40 minutes.

Mather took a party to Zanskar ('the hidden kingdom') in 1987 – the precursor to a series of increasingly exotic expeditions. As the range of School societies widened, debating flourished under Neville Clark, while the Political Society, started by Mark Peel and addressed by a series of eminent public figures, stirred up a high level of informed discussion. In 1987 the curriculum was restructured, providing wider choice at A-level and introducing drama, technology, information technology and (for a short time) vehicle design and engineering at GCSE. The relationship between A-level and Higher was further refined, and as the pace of academic change accelerated, heads of department gradually took over from hard-pressed housemasters the direction of curricular policy, leaving them and their tutors the key role of monitoring individual progress.

All these advances were making little impact on the public image of the School, and the Governors were increasingly worried. Cochrane was away from the School increasingly often as he sat on various boards and committees and in 1986 acted as commandant of the athletes' village at the Edinburgh Commonwealth Games, for which he was awarded the MBE. These duties, and the affable way he discharged them, were of some PR value to the School, but the staff wanted to see more of him in school, and prospective parents coming to visit the School were sometimes dismayed to be told they could not see the Headmaster. There were also worries over delays in decision-making and communication. His concern for the individual was, however, abundantly clear, and staff and parents found him always ready to listen to their ideas. The management team had been beefed up in 1984 by the creation of the post of Deputy Headmaster and the arrival of the ebullient Neil Henderson, whose cryptic wit and frontal approach to discipline made him an instant School character and sent shivers down the spine of would-be malefactors. It had not been easy to restore the School's reputation for strong discipline in the new age of mutual understanding.

Cochrane had made clear his dislike of corporal punishment, which finally became a thing of the past in the mid-1980s. This was in line with the trend elsewhere – an interesting one when most of the public (and many parents) went on thinking of it as the most effective deterrent, and many pupils preferred it to the long-drawn-out punishments that took its place, like gating or rustication. It was quickly over and done with. But headmasters knew that the image of the cane conjured up the bad old days in the public mind, and, above all, it did not fit the new relationship between teacher and taught. This was much closer than it had been in the past, and was based above all on reason and understanding, so something like caning which puts an end to dialogue and says 'Take that!' seemed an anachronism. In a co-educational school above all, no master (or mistress) is willing to beat a girl, so there is a glaring anomaly as long as corporal punishment continues.

As co-education fed through the system (until by 1988 girls formed 43 per cent of the School population), its civilising effects spread as prefects treated their juniors more gently and the barriers between different years came down. Full co-education also meant a girls' uniform. The startling range of girls' fashions in the 1970s gave way to uniform jumpers and kilted skirts (not too long or too short, choice of tartan permitted), with the option of a brown skirt in the summer. Boys'

Neil Henderson, appointed to the new post of Deputy Headmaster in 1984.

CCF camp officers with Cochrane in 1984.

turn-out was meanwhile improving since the ubiquitous but shapeless 'cords' had been taken out of the uniform in 1983.

The 80th anniversary of the Corps was celebrated in 1988. The contingent had shown great staying power, and under officers like Leslie Barr, Joe Hills, Neville Clark and Andrew Murray and Sergeant-Majors George McAlpine and Willy Ross, it had diversified and retained a vigorous life which many schools had lost. The same was true of the School's religious life. Even in the turbulence of the 1960s, the regular succession of morning Chapel each weekday and evening prayers in houses had not been abandoned. David Weekes provided stability and inspiration as Chaplain, while the Presbyterian presence was sustained by Norman Drummond, John Murdoch and Ronnie Selby Wright, who had originally helped devise for Fettes and Loretto the joint Confirmation service. In 1990 this was to develop into an unique and remarkable form of service where Anglicans and members of the Church of Scotland were confirmed into both Churches.

In 1987, as the Governors agonised over the School's local image and its falling numbers, Cochrane announced that he had been invited to head a new international boarding Sixth Form College in Holland and would be leaving in the summer of 1988. Compassionate and thoughtful in his personal dealings, he had, however, never fully solved the problems that dogged the School on his arrival or won over the Scottish prep schools. The School's local reputation had suffered, and

A service in the Chapel in the 1980s.

Gathering in the Old Library for the visit in 1984 of the Moderator of the Church of Scotland, the Very Revd Dr J. Fraser McLuskey.

when added to the disincentive of run-down boarding houses, this had had a bad effect on enrolment. Cochrane had, however, taken two brave steps that were crucial in securing the School's future and paving the way for its renaissance in the 1990s – the introduction of full co-education and the funding of a complete overhaul of the living accommodation by the sale of the running track area . Both these measures had to be pushed through in the face of opposition and even unpopularity, but they were an essential launch-pad for the next stage in the School's growth. He passed on to his successor a school which had radically changed its composition. It still numbered over 500 and was solvent on current account, but 43 per cent were girls and 16 per cent day pupils. It was threatened with acute funding problems, but, at the same time, it was building up to high academic standards and beginning to generate a community spirit far removed from the old days of fixed hierarchy and conformity to a rigid traditional etiquette.

Boys and girls coming from College.

9

Yesterday and Today
THYNE : 1988–98

Cometh the hour, cometh the man. Malcolm Thyne, eighth Headmaster, had known the School during his first appointment at the Edinburgh Academy. Since then he had been a highly successful housemaster at Oundle and Headmaster at St Bees, Cumbria (where he had raised the numbers from 300 to 400). When he arrived at Fettes in 1988 with his wife Eleanor (whose charm, warmth and discretion provided the ideal foil for her husband's restless energy), the job he had taken on looked daunting. He believed passionately in boarding education, but nationally, boarding numbers were declining, and at Fettes the number of boarding boys was heading down fast. Relations between the Junior School and the Senior School were awkward, and the liberal disciplinary policies of the previous 17 years, for all their admirable humanity, meant that the boys and girls were unsure what the rules were. Many were keen to have the security of a clear-cut behaviour structure, but others were happy to interpret any vagueness to their own advantage. However, although Thyne found a few 'difficult' pupils, the majority were civilised and positive, and the atmosphere generated by co-education was a warm one. The quality of the Common Room was good, and he could see at once that the School was much better than its local reputation. It was, said Andrew Murray, like a Rolls Royce with bald tyres, muddy paintwork and navigational problems, but fundamentally a machine of quality. Malcolm Thyne felt the whole School community would respond to a strong lead and clear direction, and, with the help of Lord Weir, his enthusiastic Chairman of Governors, he had every intention of providing it.

His first four years were spent sorting out policies and improving morale. Having no natural instinct to delegate, he over-worked continually. Delegation meant lack of control. Malcolm Thyne wanted to monitor the School's performance at every level, and so chaired every important committee himself. Although the method was centralized, his obvious dedication to the School and his sense of humour sugared the pill. A born administrator, he soon established a tight grip on the detail of school life. In matters of discipline, openness was the watchword. Policies and rules were laid out with great clarity, and concerns were shared with the School, and with parents at Founder's Day. He was a noticing Headmaster, and when he noticed, he acted.

'Mr Malcolm Thyne en route *from St Bees to Fettes', drawn by Trevor Green in 1988.*

Malcolm and Eleanor Thyne and the prefects outside the Lodge, 1993.

A sketch of Thyne, by Joanna Potter.

For three years numbers continued to slump. Then at last, in the autumn of 1992, the tide turned. The rolls for 1992–93 showed the long-awaited rise. One change had made a big difference: the decision in 1991 to integrate the Junior School with the main school and re-name it Inverleith House. The Head of Mathematics, Andrew Alexander, took the House over as the message went out that the staff of Senior and Junior Schools were now to be integrated, and that to be admitted to Inverleith was to be admitted to Fettes. The hurdle of Common Entrance no longer stood in the way of transfer to the Senior School. As its status changed, numbers in Inverleith shot up, from 65 in 1991 to 100 three years later.

As morale in the School improved and numbers at last bottomed out, Thyne, aided by his Deputies Neil Henderson and David Rhodes, did not relax discipline. His firm stance was not problem-free, and the expulsion of six boys in September 1992 led subsequently to a campaign to discredit the School pursued over several years by a parent of one of the expelled boys and a journalist. Newspaper editors know that stories of Toffs Behaving Badly (like those of errant clergy or royals) add spice to their pages, but this attack on the School's integrity was sustained in an extraordinary way. To the bewildered parents and pupils it was as if there were two

122

schools, the oppressive Fettes of journalistic myth, and the Fettes they knew with its warm and understanding atmosphere. John Clare of *The Daily Telegraph*, arriving in October 1995 to investigate these 'lurid tales', discovered instead that 'today's 485 boys and girls find Fettes under Mr Thyne as friendly and happy a school as any on either side of the border.' Although the impression given was in many ways appalling, the campaign had two good effects. It united the whole School community (boys, girls, staff and parents) in shared resentment at what they saw as its unfairness, and the message of strong discipline it implied was welcomed by many.

Numbers went on rising, as prospective parents liked what they saw. As, between 1988 and 1991, the proceeds of the sale of the running-track were spent on a lavish reconstruction of Moredun, Glencorse and Carrington, mothers could at long last be shown round smart, comfortable boarding houses with first-class sanitation and study bedrooms. In 1991 a new technology suite opened, and computers were installed in three separate computer rooms, followed by an all-weather games pitch in 1993, a face-lift for the School library in 1996, and the refurbishment of Kimmerghame in 1996–97. The biggest development, however, was at Inverleith House, where a new boarding wing, assembly hall and classrooms were completed in 1995, to cope with the rising demand at this level. The Government's new league tables had made parents far more conscious of examination success, and here the School was surging ahead. In 1993 and 1994, the A-level pass rate was 100 per cent, and the proportion of A grade passes was high, rising in 1997 to a remarkable 54 per cent, while at GCSE the upward momentum of the 1980s was extended. The curriculum had become very broad, with 19 subjects on offer at GCSE, 18 at A level and 18 at Higher, not to speak of the fashionable 'core skills'. The School's best advertisement, however, was the ordinary Fettesian, friendly, articulate and (as

The modernised Glencorse House is re-opened by Crichton-Miller on 29th May 1990.

A girls' hockey match against Glenalmond on the all-weather pitch, opened in 1993.

123

a parent told one newspaper) distinguished by 'confidence without arrogance'.

The strong academic tone was matched by the School's vivid cultural life. Drama flowered in a sequence of remarkable productions like Brendan Butler's *Oedipus Rex* of 1992, the first of a series of Fettes plays to be taken on to the Festival Fringe. These were warmly received and even included a house play, Betty Thomson's *The Prime of Miss Jean Brodie*, and *Equus*, directed by two members of the Lower Sixth. The choral recitals and concerts staged by Richard Brett and David Thomas showed extraordinary quality, and the exploding range of paintings, drawings and ceramics generated in the art rooms by John Darmody's team completed the picture of a rich aesthetic life, reflected in *The Fettesian*, more than ever an immensely professional production. The sheer range of activities and societies meant that the life of a boarder could be hectically busy, and as exams approached, the multi-talented had to make hard choices about their priorities to make space for the vital revision. The essence of the Fettes of the 1990s, though, was the sense of community within the School. This was strengthened by weekend social events at all levels, by buffet suppers in the Headmaster's Lodge, and, for staff, by Guest

Below left: *the 1997 School play,* Much Ado About Nothing; *below right: publicity for Fettes' two plays at the Edinburgh Festival Fringe in 1994.*

The group expedition to Mt Fettes in New Zealand in 1995, the College's 125th anniversary.

Nights and the Christmas Ball. Boys and girls from Europe and further afield were quickly absorbed into the School, and gave a non-parochial, cosmopolitan flavour to the atmosphere.

The Year 1995 was the School's 125th anniversary. The occasion was marked by an expedition to New Zealand led by Andrew Murray to climb the School's eponymous mountain. The top of Mount Fettes, first discovered and named in 1887 by Charles Douglas, a relation of Sir William, was duly reached by Fiona O'Reilly and Alex Michie, backed by an enthusiastic team. It was also the 25th anniversary of the first admission of a girl to Fettes, and as such a good moment to acknowledge the success of co-education. In 1992 Julia Close had been appointed the first girl Head of School, and the event provoked no reaction like the reported remark of the Rugbeian when Rugby appointed its first girl Head of School in 1995: 'She can't expect to have our respect when she's not in the 1st XV.' By now the appointment seemed natural, if not inevitable, and was soon followed by that of Camilla Stack. The opening in 1993 of the all-weather pitch named after Ian Sutcliffe gave a further boost to the standard of girls' games, and they were soon matching the best in Scotland at lacrosse, hockey and tennis. A select band was even introduced to rugby by Christopher Carruthers and played in the first inter-school girls' rugby match in Scotland against the Edinburgh Academy. The successful lacrosse and hockey tour to Japan and Australia in 1997 was a further assertion of the status of girls' games. They were showing the same vigour and professionalism as the boys', where rugby and cricket teams were holding their own in a very tough circuit, helped by Thyne's appointment of a series of young masters with coaching skills, and rugby tours to South Africa and Hong Kong.

Boy–girl relations had normalized since the early days when Sixth Form girls were viewed as sex objects suddenly appearing to excite the hormones. The matter-

The girls' rugby team in 1995.

125

of-fact atmosphere of mature co-education meant fewer bursts of unbridled passion. When Thyne posted a ban on 'public displays of affection' in 1989, it was almost welcomed by the pupils as confirmation of a stereotypical adult attitude, and gleefully reinterpreted as a 'six-inch rule'. This regulation, which existed only in the folklore, satisfied their longing to believe that adults were pedantic enough to specify an exact permissible distance between boy and girl.

One of the great successes of the Thyne era was the advance in the ideal of leadership. Prefectship, with its rather patchy history, was not to be abolished but transformed. Leadership training was begun for School prefects, and spread to others aspiring to any sort of leadership. It was accompanied by a change in the way people perceive leadership, as responsibility was stressed rather than privilege. Good leadership is crucial in diminishing unkindness and establishing civilised values, and, to ensure that the community respected its own leaders, School prefects were appointed only after full discussion and sounding out of opinion throughout the School.

Parents of today, faced with the colossal cost of sending a child to boarding

The new wing of Inverleith House, completed in 1995.

school, understandably want to find out how likely it is that the school they have in mind will deliver results. In the last decade they have begun to shop around, guides and exam league tables in hand. Schools have had to sell themselves and set up more and more elaborate publicity machines. At Fettes, there was a steady increase in dialogue with parents, as special seminars for parents were held, parental questionnaires issued, and (from 1991) annual Open Days held. Meanwhile, a tide of paper was engulfing the desks of school heads as more and more external guidelines and directives arrived, devoted to the pursuit of quality assurance. Education has been increasingly infiltrated by the techniques devised in the world of industry, and during the 1990s development plans, audits, teacher appraisals, handbooks and job descriptions proliferated. Much that was previously assumed had now to be specified.

The way the School had kept ahead of all this helped when a School Inspection was announced for 1995. Afterwards, its report made pleasing reading for Malcolm Thyne and the School. The response from parents to the Inspection questionnaire had revealed an extraordinary level of support. The Inspectors credited the School with ten key strengths (an unusually high number). These included the favourable staff–pupil ratio, the tutorial system and the exam results, the courtesy and behaviour of the pupils, the hard-working, caring staff, the range of activities, the opportunities for personal and social development and the encouragement given to individual strengths and talents. Most welcome of all was the high praise given to the staff–pupil and pupil–pupil relationships, and the pastoral care. It was an objective endorsement of the quality of the atmosphere that envelopes visitors when they walk into the Fettes of today – warm and relaxed, yet inquiring and dynamic.

In the summer of 1997, as a new business plan was unveiled under Lord Maclean, the new Chairman of Governors, Malcolm Thyne announced he would retire in 1998. He had reached his target figure for the pupil population, and the School's health was obvious. Since 1991, numbers had risen by 20 per cent at a time when the independent boarding sector nationally had declined, and the School was now the largest independent boarding school in Scotland. The finances were secure at last, and an excellent work ethic had been established. That year, 15 Fettesians gained entry to Oxford or Cambridge and, of the A-levels, 76 per cent were at A or B – a result unrivalled since the start of A-levels at the School. Even this was surpassed by the 89 per cent rate in 1998, Malcom Thyne's final year. His own contribution in galvanising a gifted staff and winning the confidence of parents is hard to overstate. He had given the School once more a confident belief in itself and its future.

The recent accession of a Labour Government had meant the imminent death of the Assisted Places Scheme, but it also meant a Fettesian Prime Minister. There had been a series of distinguished Fettesian parliamentarians in the past, but when Tony Blair arrived in 10 Downing Street in May 1997, he was the first to reach the supreme office of state. Other Fettesians have made their own very different impact on the society of the late 20th century, often in ways little noticed, and alongside the captains of industry, the journalists and the holders of university chairs are those

Malcolm Thyne.

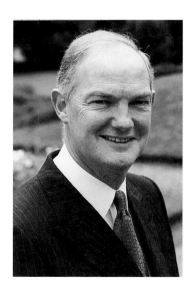

whose work has been with the less privileged like the three Fettesians who led the Iona Community between 1967 and 1995.

The elusive imprint of a school on those who pass through it is hard to trace, whether they end up as Prime Minister, accountant or social worker. But their qualities embody the real strengths of any school, whether they found their schooldays inspiring, dull, challenging, traumatic or idyllic. This is the hidden dimension of a school history. In 1912 Ian Hay, boy and master at Fettes, wrote:

> Just as the sun never sets upon the British Empire, so it never sets upon the Old Boys of a great public school at once. They are gone out into all lands; they are upholding the honour of the School all the world over.

Such a reflection is seldom conscious, but nostalgia can strike at unlikely times and places, as once it struck Will Ogilvy, boy at Fettes and then jackeroo on a New South Wales sheepfarm, who, sitting under a gum-tree in the outback in 1893, wrote a poem on the back of his copy of *The Fettesian*, putting into the simple rhythms of Longfellow's *Hiawatha* his sense of a boyhood past, of something lost:

> And we sometimes see in dreaming
> All the corridors of Fettes . . .
> And we wake, and are unhappy,
> For those merry days are over.

Such dreams are often bitter-sweet, but they have the sharp, authentic taste of youth.

EPILOGUE

In the autumn of 1998 Michael Spens became the ninth Headmaster of Fettes, to lead the School into the new millennium. A graduate in Natural Sciences, Michael continues a trend which started with Malcolm Thyne, the first scientist to be Headmaster. Educated at Marlborough and Selwyn College, Cambridge, he has worked in marketing with United Biscuits and taught in New Zealand, but the majority of his teaching life so far has been spent at Radley, where he became Senior Housemaster as well as coaching the 1st XV and taking charge of golf, rock-climbing and the Mountaineering Club. He has also run in two London Marathons. Most recently, Michael has served with distinction as Headmaster of Caldicott in Buckinghamshire. He brings with him his wife Deborah and their three young children, who seem set to make their own impact on Fettes life, and his appointment promises a continuing surge forward in the School's reputation and the quality of its communal life. A new and exciting chapter begins.

The Spens family.

CHRONOLOGY

1836   Death of Sir William Fettes.

1870   School opens (School House and Moredun House, then called Glencorse, only), October 5.

1872   Gymnasium and Chapel completed, April.
Carrington House (then called Dalmeny) opened, June.

1873   Glencorse House opened, September.
Moredun Crescent built.

1875   Numbers reach 200.

1878   *The Fettesian* first published, April.

1879   Modern Side started.

1881   'Floreas Fettesia' first sung.

1883   Outbreak of diphtheria, migration of School to Windermere.
Death of Mrs Potts.
Kimmerghame House opened at 6, Moredun Crescent, September.

1886   Educational Endowments Commission hands the School over to Governors instead of Trustees.

1889   Death of Dr Potts.
Appointment of Revd William Augustus Heard as second Headmaster.

1890   Swimming baths burnt down and re-built.

1896   Fire in old laboratories.

1897   New laboratories opened.

1904   Death of John Yeo, Housemaster of Carrington.

1906   Cricket pavilion completed.

1908   Officers Training Corps started in School.

1912   First appearance of Pipe Band.

1919   Retirement of Heard, succeeded by Alec Ashcroft.

1920   Kimmerghame re-opened in Moredun Crescent.
Central heating installed in College.

1921   War Memorial unveiled, October.

1924   Fettesian-Lorettonian Boys Club opened in St Giles Street.

1926   Young's Field laid out.

1927   Golf Course opened, May.

1928   New Kimmerghame House opened, September.

1939   Scottish Leaving Certificate abandoned in favour of Oxford & Cambridge Certificate.
Bomb-proof shelters built in front of College.
Air raid over Fettes grounds, October.

1940   Top hats and tails abolished.
Kimmerghame House requisitioned by Government, boys moved to Glencorse.

1943   First summer harvest camp at Ceres, Fife.

1945   Retirement of Ashcroft, succeeded by Donald Crichton-Miller.

1946   Kimmerghame House re-opened with 64 boys, September.
School numbers reach 300.
Schoolhouse divided into College East and College West.

1949   New school uniform.

1950   Fettesian-Lorettonian Boys Club moves to Crewe Toll.
Chapel re-opened to take whole School.
Lower Dining-Hall opened.

1951   Inverleith (waiting house) opened.

1952   First Commemoration week-end.
Fire on top floor of Carrington.
New gymnasium opened.

1953   Concert Hall completed.

1954 New running track opened.
1955 Visit of HM the Queen and the Duke of Edinburgh.
Music and Art School opened.
1956 New dress regulations.
1957 New Science laboratories opened.
1958 Crichton-Miller appointed HM of Stowe, succeeded by Dr Ian McIntosh.
1962 New class-rooms and CCF huts erected.
1963 Fire in Carrington (study area).
First half-term holiday.
Comely Bank Nursery bought for City Police.
1965 First joint concert with girls of St George's.
Old Tuck Shop demolished.
1966 New Dining Hall opened.
1967 Fire in Glencorse.
Arniston House opened.
Sanatorium moved to back of College.
New Library created in old Dining-Hall.
1968 Moredun Crescent demolished.
West Woods houses built.
1970 Centenary. Celebrations and visit of Queen Mother to open new Science School.
Publication of *100 Years of Fettes, Fettes Register 1870–1970* and *Fettesian Centenary Supplement.*
First girl arrives.
1971 Retirement of McIntosh, succeeded by Anthony Chenevix-Trench.
College West and College East amalgamate.
1973 Junior school opened in Malcolm House and old Sanatorium.
1976 Numbers reach 500.
1977 Cafeteria system introduced at lunch.

1979 Death of Chenevix-Trench. Cameron Cochrane becomes Headmaster.
1981 Arniston closes for boys.
1982 Arniston re-opens for girls.
Part of golf course sold for development.
1983 First two women Governors appointed.
Fettes 2000 Appeal launched.
1984 Schoolhouse closes for boys, re-opens for girls.
Dalmeny House started as Sixth Form house for day girls.
Appointment of first Deputy Headmaster.
New boarding facility opened at Junior School.
1987 West section of Golf Course and running track sold for development.
1988 Cochrane appointed to Prinz Willem-Alexander College, succeeded by Malcolm Thyne.
Schoolhouse divided again.
1991 Junior School integrated with Senior School to become Inverleith House.
1995 125th anniversary, 25th anniversary of girls.
A History of Sir Willam Fettes and *A Nest of Singing Birds* (Fettes poets) published.
Mount Fettes (in New Zealand) climbed.
1996 Link with Ying Hao school in China established.
1997 Fettes tartan created.
First Fettesian Prime Minister elected to office.
1998 Retirement of Malcolm Thyne, succeeded by Michael Spens.

INDEX